THE SOUL IN PARAPHRASE

PRAYER AND THE RELIGIOUS AFFECTIONS

DON E SALIERS

OSL Publications
Cleveland, Ohio

The Soul in Paraphrase:
Prayer and the Religious Affections
(Second Edition)

ISBN 1-878009-09-5

This book is printed on acid-free paper that meets the American National Standards Institute Z39.48 Standard

Produced and manufactured in the United States of America by
OSL Publications
The publishing ministry of the Order of Saint Luke
5246 Broadway
Cleveland, Ohio 44127-1500

Production Editing: Timothy J. Crouch, O.S.L.

The book cover was inspired by the Lindesfarne Gospels, an 8th century English manuscript, and was designed by C. E. Visminas Co., Ltd., purveyors of worship bulletins and Christian education materials from our Christian heritage. For a catalog call (800) 752-1429, or write P.O. Box 10189, 812 Ivy Street, Pittsburgh, PA 15232.

The Order of Saint Luke is a Religious Order in the United Methodist Church, dedicated to sacramental and liturgical scholarship, education and practice. The purpose of the publishing ministry is to put into the hands of students and practitioners resources which have theological, historical, ecumenical and practical integrity.

CONTENTS

Acknowledgments i

Preface to the second edition iii

1. Religious Affections Revisited 1

2. Prayer as the Language of the Heart 17

3. Prayer: Shaping and Expressing Emotion .. 29

4. The Christian Affections 40
    Gratitude and Giving Thanks 40
    Holy Fear and Repentance........................ 48
    Joy and Suffering 53
    Love of God and Neighbor.....................56

5. Praying and Thinking:
   The Work of Theology................................. 60

6. Praying and Being:
   Responding to the World 72

7. Praying with Christ:
   Signs of Living Prayer............................ 87

Afterword 99

Notes 103

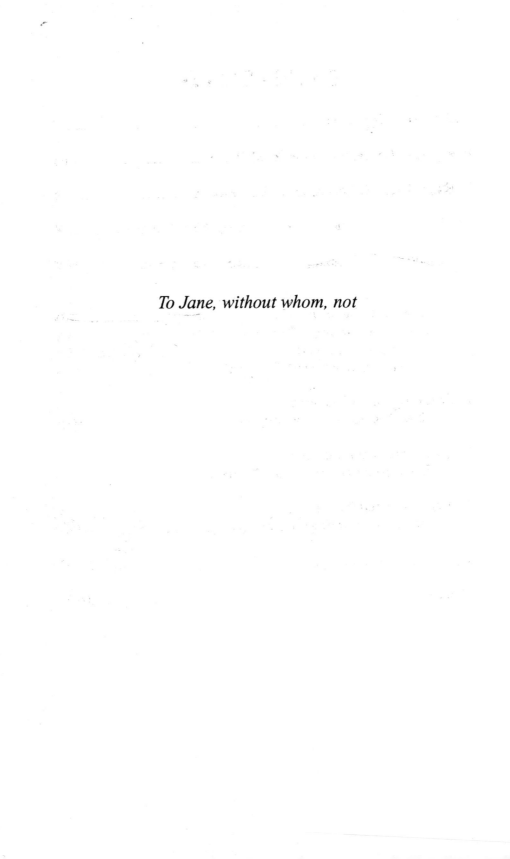

To Jane, without whom, not

Acknowledgements

This book has everged from my preoccupation with relations between prayer, theology, and Christian spirituality over a number of years. Seminars at Yale Divinity School, the University of Notre Dame, and Candler School of Theology, Emory University, form a significant part of the matrix of reflection expressed in these pages. To those students and colleagues I am grateful for nurture, witting and unwitting, of my own theological insights.

Most of the writing was accomplished on sabbatical leave in 1977-1978 during which I was a Fellow of the Institute for Ecumenical and Cultural Research, St. John's Abbey and University, Collegeville, Minnesota. I am indebted to Dr. and Mrs. Robert Bilheimer, Sr. Dolores Schuh, and to Fr. Kilian McDonnell of the Institute for providing such a hospitable environment for my work there and kindness to my household through a vigorous Minnesota winter.

I wish to thank Fr. Colman Barry, O.S.B., Director of the Institute for Spirituality at St. John's, at whose kind invitation I addressed a conference in March, 1978, with material incorporated into the final chapter of this book. Parts of chapter five first appeared as an essay entitled, "Theology and Prayer: Some Conceptual Reminders," in *Worship* (April, 1974); and a version of chapter three was given as an address to the Conference on Prayer sponsored by the Murphy Center for Liturgical Research at the University of Notre Dame, subsequently published in *Worship* (October, 1975) and in *Christians at Prayer*, edited by John Gallen, S.J. (Notre Dame: University of Notre Dame Press, 1977).

Nor could this book have been written without a sabbatical leave provided by Emory University and a grant from the Association of Theological Schools, the Andrew W. Mellon Foundation, and the Arthur Vining Davis Foundation. For their encouragement and support I am deeply grateful.

I acknowledge with special gratitude the constant and fine editorial sense of Justus George Lawler under whose surveillance this work took final shape. To Michael Miller and most especially to Ms. Marilyn Wilborn, whose assistance in preparing the manuscript was invaluable and unfailingly gracious, my sincere thanks.

Quotations from the Bible follow the text of the Revised Standard Version. Grateful acknowledgment is made to Oxford University Press, at

Clarendon Press, for permission to quote George Herbert's "Prayer" from *The Works of George Herbert,* edited by F.E. Hutchinson (1941).

The expanded section of the "Afterword" is adapted from "On the Distinctiveness of Christian Emotions" which appeared in *Weavings*, Vol. VI, No. 3 (May/June, 1991).

Preface
to the Second Edition

Since this book first took shape, I am more than ever convinced that prayer is central to Christian life and theology, and that the struggle to pray authentically in this age takes us deep into the emotional depths of what it is to be human.

Indeed, the life of prayer is itself a double journey into the reality of God and, at the same time, into the depths of our common humanity. Such a journey, once begun, shapes and expresses the emotions. These pages attempt to show how such formation in a particular pattern of religious affections is theological and not merely "subjective" or experiential. For the Christian life is itself "love of God and neighbor, grief about one's own waywardness, joy in the merciful salvation of our god, gratitude, hope, and peace."[1] Thus, to say we love God but without love of neighbor, or to speak of God without gratitude or pain over injustice and suffering is not to have understood how prayer, experience and theology are related.

In her wise little volume, *To Love As God Loves*, Roberta Bondi, writing in conversation with the early monastic mothers and fathers, writes: "Being a Christian means learning to love with God's love. But God's love is not a warm feeling in the pit of the stomach. It has definite characteristics we learn in the course of our life . . .as we ponder over what we can say about God as God deals with us, and . . .as we model our own lives on what we have learned."[2] The "definite characteristics" of religious affections, and specifically of Christian affections, are the very stuff of theology. Hence, George Herbert's "Prayer" has been, and continues to be, a touchstone to my continuing explorations. For the connections between praying and the whole range of human life before God has to do with "sounding heav'n and earth;" as well as "something understood."

This book reappears now amidst a veritable flood of books on prayer and spirituality. At the same time, the popular literature on dealing and coping with emotions has reached a crescendo. So, in addition to the more classical issues dealt with in the first two chapters and throughout these pages, I am increasingly aware of the issues generated by the collisions between the two literatures just mentioned. While the basic themes and argument of the book remain the same, I sense the need to address the contemporary context more directly.

There is a question, perhaps a cluster of questions, which haunts anyone who seeks to live a deeper Christian life in a culture which has been profoundly shaped by psychological theories and therapies. "Why do you always talk about certain emotions when you know that an ordinary person finds them impossible to sustain?" "How do we know that religious experiences and the affections aren't self-deceptions?" These questions come, not from a cynical skeptic, but from a genuinely concerned person who has been raised in the Church. Talk about emotions such as love and joy struck her as hopelessly ideal or radically ambiguous. Her questions catch the fact that Christians are called to a life that is distinctive and that "holiness" has to do with the depth of love, hope, repentance and joy. But her questions also reveal a dilemma we must face: The Christian language of the heart, so central to the psalms and the Bible and to the reality of prayer, is suspect. Suspect by those who find religious practices infantile, or who have come to see so much oppression and in the very appeal to such affections. This has been brought forcefully to our attention by both feminist and liberationist theologians. The task of listening to and replying to the objections from feminist and liberationist thinkers remains to a future book. Nevertheless a few words about the questions posed above may help set a new context for the inquiry at hand.

The language of faith is the language of emotion, but it is much more than "feeling states." Much religious practice has indeed led to emotional suppression and oppression in the name of God. More subtle has been the too-easy identification of certain culturally-dominant patterns of dealing with emotions with the ideals of the Christian life. So gratitude and thanksgiving have often been preached without any attention to the need to deal with lamentation, anger, and the very wrestling with God which characterizes the Scriptures, especially the psalms.

That there are abuses of human emotional life in the name of prayer and religious discipline should not surprise us, however. This is because the language of faith requires emotional vulnerability. The spiritual life is itself a passion for God and hence opens up the abyss and the ecstacy of the human. One of the most basic root metaphors in Hebrew and Christian Scriptures is the human heart at full stretch. In what follows we consider how faith expresses itself in its deepest longings, hopes, joys and fears: "My heart overflows with a goodly theme;" "Create in me a clean heart, O God;" "You shall love the Lord your God with all your heart, and with all your soul, and with all your might;" or "the heart is deceitful . . .who can understand it?" or "but Mary kept all these things, pondering them in her heart." Throughout all the biblical literature the heart is the center of a human life. To characterize the heart is to say what a human being is by calling attention to how the world is experienced and regarded. Pharoah's heart was hardened: but the grace of God "gladdens the heart." Human beings have "stony hearts," but God desires to give us "hearts of flesh" and to write divine law "upon our hearts."

The language of the heart as the seat of the affections *and* the understanding is thus indispensable and authoritative in Scripture because it gives us a way of speaking about what is deepest and most complex about human beings. Is it any wonder, then, that the language of faith is also the language of the heart? This helps us understand why we could describe the whole of the Christian life as a set of deep affections, and a pattern of being in the world gratefully, joyfully, peacefully, compassionately. By "affections" I mean a basic attunement toward the world which is the spring of our being and our acting. Affections are not mere feeling states we have from time to time, but are the specific ways we perceive the world in and through a "sense" of the world. So it is understandable that the New Testament literature speaks of putting away the works of the flesh and of cultivating the fruits of the Spirit instead. Not jealousy and anger and envy, but love and joy and kindness. Not the passions and desires we have when left to our own devices, but those affections which flow from walking in the Spirit. Yet this is just where difficult questions emerge.

Many contemporary people, well-schooled in Freud or secular psychological thought, find the whole question of religious experience and the cultivation of certain emotions suspect from the beginning. If religious faith itself is regarded as infantile or as essentially repressive, then any talk about the heart and affections in terms of the lists of the fruits of the Spirit will be dismissed as humanly immature. It is often said that the judgments and reasoning of religious believers are distorted by their emotions. "Be reasonable, don't let your emotions sway your judgment!" If religious beliefs are regarded as projections out of insecurity or anxiety, then the affections which are given shape by those beliefs are but the trembling of such human insecurities. Of course God can easily become an excuse for simply believing what is already comfortable and illusory. Should this lead us to regard as distorted all affections connected with religious belief in God? This counterquestion we leave for now. The problem of sustaining hope, love, or gentleness is, on the other hand, part of the struggle to live faithfully - to pray and to become prayerful.

Prayer the Churches banquet, Angels age,
    God's breath in man returning to his birth,
    The soul in paraphrase, heart in pilgrimmage,
The Christian plummet sounding heav'n and earth;
Engine against th' Almightie, sinners towre,
    Reversed thunder, Christ-side-piercing spear,
    The six-daies world transposing in an houre,
A kind of tune, which all things heare and fear;
Softnesse, and peace, and joy, and love, and blisse,
    Exalted Manna, gladnesse of the best,
    Heaven in ordinarie, man well drest,
The milkie way, the bird of Paradise,
    Church-bels beyond the starres heard, the souls bloud,
    The land of spices; something understood.

George Herbert, from *The Temple*

one
Religious Affections Revisited

Leo Tolstoy, in his autobiographical essay entitled "A Confession," tells of a friend who stopped believing in the Christian faith.

> On a hunting expedition, when he was already twenty-six, he once, at the place where they put up for the night, knelt down in the evening to pray - a habit retained from childhood. His elder brother, who was at the hunt with him, was lying on some hay and watching him. When the younger man had finished and was settling down for the night, his brother said to him: "So you still do that?" They said nothing more to one another. But from that day he ceased to say his prayers or go to church. And now he has not prayed, received communion, or gone to church for thirty years. And this was not because he knows his brother's convictions and has joined him in them, nor because he has decided anything in his own soul, but simply because the word spoken by his brother was like the push of a finger on a wall that was ready to fall by its own weight.[1]

For many this story's point seems remarkably true to contemporary experience. Carefully preserved piety sometimes seems a house of cards, when someone asks, "So you still do that?" Or we may suddenly catch ourselves at prayer, saying the old familiar religious words, and it may strike us that these are empty gestures. The questions then flood in upon us: What on earth are we doing in these acts, with this language — what are we saying, and what do we mean? The vulnerability of praying stands revealed, its intimate relation to religious belief unveiled.

In recent times there has been an unprecedented reawakening of interest in prayer across a broad spectrum of church traditions. Prayer groups, both inside and outside established churches, are attracting increasing numbers. Many seek without knowing what they will find; others testify to powerful experiences with God the Holy Spirit. Side by side with the charismatic renewal are diverse movements of the ''spiritual life,'' some of which show little awareness of liturgical prayer. Then, too, the changes in liturgical prayer within Roman Catholic and Protestant traditions have brought a new awareness of pluralism in prayer forms. For many, the loss of uniformity in liturgical prayer has been confusing. For others, the variety has been a refreshing discovery. Consequently, many of us are struggling to understand the meaning and point of prayer in relation to traditional theology as well as to the unsettling forces in contemporary experience.

Questions and confusion are generated within the churches and in the cultures at large. The most troubling questions bear directly upon relationships between prayer, religious experience, and theology. The issues this book addresses are occasioned as much by religious awakening as they are by the onslaught of skepticism. Even those who have undergone Tolstoy's question may continue to have strong religious concerns. To such readers, too, this book is addressed, since the difficulty of prayer in their case is linked with the *absence* of sense and reality in a now discarded habit of praying.

My intention, however, is not simply to present an *apologia* for prayer in our day - a timely tract. Rather, in addressing questions and misunderstandings forced upon us in the current situation, I wish to uncover themes and issues which belong to theological reflection in any age. The recovery of personal and experiential dimensions of religious faith often brings with it an anti-doctrinal bias. Many who claim extraordinary experiences claim that personal transformation and encounter with God have little to do with doctrines or theology. Lines are drawn between experience and doctrine, between feeling and thinking, between emotion and thought. Such stark contrasts are not new in the history of prayer or of theology. At the same time, theologically reflective people have been known to harbor an abiding distrust of religious experience. In the contemporary world, awareness of how prayer and worship can be abused by religious hucksters to manipulate emotions and feeling may deepen such distrust and lead to a stress on intellectually respectable doctrines and faith. Fear of ''emotionalism'' and distaste for what is considered the vulgarity of emotional display reinforce such attitudes. In either case sharp contrasts are drawn between experience and doctrine.

The current renewal of interest in extraordinary religious experiences generates a need to understand more clearly what is meant by ''experience'' in various claims and counterclaims. Popular articles such as "Are We a Nation of Mystics?"[2] have brought the topic into everyday household conversation. While the interest in "peak experiences" and religious feeling is not always connected directly with prayer and worship, the correlation is unmistakable. This book addresses the relation between prayer and emotion, considering prayer in both its widest sense and its specific types. The range of what we call praying must be taken into account: liturgical and devotional, communal and individual, spontaneous and formulated, active and contemplative. So also with emotions and experience; some of the puzzlements and misunderstandings in appeals to religious experiences need to be untangled. This requires thinking about differences between emotions, feelings, and moods, and tracing out the patterns of human affections involved in various modes of prayer.

Many people find the whole question of prayer embarrassing. This is because the most threatening and promising aspects of religious belief are involved. The question of prayer raises the personal issue of religious faith. Faith, Martin Luther remarked with conscious hyperbole, is prayer and nothing but prayer. Prayer is a threat and an embarrassment precisely because the most intimate and most definite features of believing in God are involved in learning to pray.

Even more to the point, many religious people may accept prayer as part of the required practices of religion without ever realizing its nature as encounter and as journey. To pray is to encounter, and to journey into, the mystery of God; at the same time to pray is to encounter the ambiguous reality of our own humanity before God. Such double encounter and journey can be dangerous. There are abusive, even demonic, prayer and worship. As Jacques Ellul and others have vigorously reminded us, prayer can be a dangerous deceit, full of human illusion.[3] One way of coping with this disquieting feature of the life of prayer is to concentrate primarily on believing the right doctrines, or in assenting to an infallible Bible, or to obediently fulfilling the duties and obligations of accepted formulas for prayer and correct behavior. Still another way is to quit religious practices entirely.

There are also people, as we have noted above, who are tired of academic doctrine and blind submission to church authorities, and who wish their religion to be full of feeling and enthusiastic commitment; they often simply embrace the Dionysian freedom of spontaneous prayer. This is a consistent tendency in pietistic movements of the past and the present. The Wesleys and a great portion of American revivalism all protested the rationalism and spiritual aridity of Protestant theology and church practice. The new prayer movements within Roman Catholicism in our day also lament the lack of spiritual zeal and personal experience in ecclesiastical forms of worship and behavior. Yet, what begins as a corrective to a heavily rational approach to theology and religious practice soon makes reflective faith suspect. What so often has begun in pietism as a legitimate revival and renewal produces, within a generation or two, a deformation of spirituality. This deformation is to be found in the substitution of sentiment and the interior consolations of experience for the more enduring affections which are the wellspring of emotion, thought, and action. Ironically, such deformation cuts the link between the experiential and doctrinal features of mature faith.

Both the rationalist and the piestistic approaches to prayer share the same error - perhaps innocently but decisively. Each is based upon the conviction that belief and emotion, that doctrine and piety, are separate concerns. If there is a connection at all in these views, it may be only external or casual: "right belief produces right feelings," *or* "true experience causes right theology." These are natural but grave mistakes which lead to misunderstandings and confusions about prayer, both corporate and individual. Misunderstanding prayer breeds impoverished theology. Ambiguities in our use of the concepts of prayer and experience are often difficult to detect. So many of us seek simple answers, and are impatient with complexity. Prayer may be profoundly simple, yet we who pray are exceedingly complex.

By this attempt to clarify some of the misunderstandings we face, I wish neither to deny nor to suppress experience in religious faith. Some readers may even find too much stress on experiential religion here for either their taste or their theology. But unfortunately, many regard *thinking* about religious experience tantamount to denying the validity of specific experiences. Any attempt to analyze religious emotions seems to destroy them, or to "rationalize" that which can only be felt and testified to. The mere having of experiences as such, however, can never guarantee truthfulness in matters of faith, doctrine, and life. Not everyone who utters "Lord, Lord!" will enter the kingdom. In fact, having intense experiences may not involve deep emotions as defined in this book. The mere having of extraordinary experiences may not lead to anything extraordinary at all.

There are, of course, particular experiences which completely reorient an entire life's thinking, feeling and acting. William James' *Varieties of Religious Experience* and much current popular religious literature present many examples of the "twice born." But not all or even most cases of converting experiences are indeed converting. This is also true of experiences belonging to the sanctification of life. Problems of self- deception and of inadequate connections between episodic experiences and the ongoing stream of life constantly recur. "Spiritual awakenings" within Christianity have always occasioned such problems. The religious situation which is the context of this book shows certain affinities to that which generated Jonathan Edwards' *Treatise Concerning Religious Affections* during the 1730's and 40's in England. Though we are not preoccupied with disputes over nature and grace and divine election, questions of how to discern the work of God the Holy Spirit have once again emerged. Increasingly, many serious thinkers are caught between those who claim religious experience to be the primary source of life and doctrine, and those who reject religious emotions and feelings either in the name of theological orthodoxy or because zealous experiential religion is regarded as vulgar.

In large measure, this book is a search for a language by which to describe and understand, so far as possible, the intricate connections between self, world, and God which are the heart of Christian prayer. Put in another way, we are concerned with the grammar of the religious affections in the context of prayer and life. Inherited ways of speaking, whether psychological, theological, or common sense, often prove inadequate or misleading in accounting for the relationships between prayer and patterns of religious experience. One thinks, for example, of our natural inclination to speak of "objective" rites and language and "subjective" feelings or states of faith. We are tempted to defend "emotion" over against reason," or the "will" against "understanding," or to exalt one and subordinate the other. I hope, therefore, to correct the misleading aspects of such easy dichotomies inherited from the past. My task is to think clearly and afresh about prayer and religious affections so as to invite a more unified vision of them.

By concentrating on the meaning and point of praying in its various modes, I take up a double task: to defend the importance of religious affections against those holding them in ill repute and to provide ways of distinguishing deep emotions which define the Christian life from mere sentiment or from passing enthusiasms. Many persons seek a way out of the dominant either/or: either the rush of enthusiasm and experiential intensity or the rationalism of fundamentalist approaches to correct doctrines about Scripture, prayer, and the church.

Readers may wonder at my choice of the term "affection." This term is, after all, a bit quaint in many circles and even obsolete. "Affection" is commonly used to mean passing sentiment, a mere "liking." But like the term "passion," it deserves to be reclaimed from the shoddiness of contemporary English usage.

As I shall emphasize, "affection" avoids some of the problems connected with the term "emotion." In everyday life we are inclined to use "emotion" to refer to feelings, moods, sudden sensations, and a wide range of other states. The word simply covers too much. For some readers, it evokes numerous competing theories of emotion, whereas "affection" is a less technical and theory-laden term. The concept of affection designates a basic attunement which lies at the heart of a person's way of being and acting. In quite specific ways, our affections qualify our perceptions, our fundamental attitudes, and our behavior; yet affections cannot be reduced to feelings, perceptions, or attitudes. Not every affection is rooted in the center of one's self with equal force or comprehensiveness, as I will make clear in exploring different patterns of affection belonging to the activity of praying.

On the one hand, then, the phrase "the affections," is used to denote a comprehensive phenomenon of life by which we understand the world *in and through* a "sense" of the world. Affections thus always combine evaluative knowledge of the world and self awareness. On the other hand, there are specific affections quite distinguishable from each other. In our everyday life we learn to mark these differences without much difficulty, and certainly without having a systematic theory of the affections. Particular affections are what they are by virtue of their objects and the characteristic roles they play in the pattern of our thought and behavior. They may show affinities with each other, or opposition and tension. Love and gladness often keep company, whereas love and fear are ordinarily in conflict. But these common sense insights may not always be true, for the ordering of our affections depends upon the complex weave of our concepts, inclinations, and judgments. The affections which are found at the center of our lives are necessarily tied to how we describe and assess the world. To be affected by human suffering and moved to compassion, for example, is to have seen the world differently from the person who is not moved. The narratives of life in which the concepts of suffering and compassion occur give us a grip on existence and tell us their significance.

There is, I am convinced, a pattern of particular affections which constitutes and governs the life of the Christian. This is the focal point of the explorations which follow.

These explorations are not intended to be exhaustive; yet they suggest an extended and more comprehensive way of understanding correlations between modes of prayer and worship and the defining dispositions of the heart. By tracing the affections of gratitude, holy fear and penitence, joy andsuffering, and love of God and neighbor, we discern the way in which doctrine and experience require one another. Showing concretely how they are ordered in the Christian life constitutes the burden of chapter four.

Jonathan Edwards, unfairly known for his sermon, "Sinners in the Hands of an Angry God," responding to questions generated in the midst of that extraordinary religious phenomenon known as the Great Awakening, writes in his *Treatise Concerning Religious Affections*

> Take away all love and hatred, all hope and fear, all anger, zeal, and affectionate desire, and the world would be in a great measure motionless and dead; there would be no such things as activity amongst mankind, or any earnest pursuit whatsoever. . . .And as in worldly things worldly affections are very much the spring of men's motion and action; so in religious matters the spring of their actions is very much religious affection; he that has doctrinal knowledge and speculation only, without affection, never is engaged in the business of religion.[4]

Edwards poses a fundamental question: What is the nature of true religion, or authentic faith? Since, for Edwards, true religion consists principally in the holy affections, he is concerned to distinguish gracious and saving affections from the mere appearances of what he calls "counterfeit religion." He is not advancing apologetics on behalf of religious feeling, as Friedrich Schleiermacher was to do a hundred years later. Rather, in the course of reflection Edwards undertakes a double task: to defend the necessity and centrality of affections against those holding emotion in ill repute, and to provide criteria for determining true and holy affections from a wide variety of emotional excesses and enthusiasms.

Surprisingly enough, for Edwards the degree of truthfulness in religious faith is not found in the experiential abundance of emotion and feeling. Like others in the Catholic and Anglican traditions who also speak of the need for experience in knowing God, he came to see that intensity of religious experience easily leads to self-deception, or to an outright contradiction of the aim of religious conversion. Instead, Edwards emphasizes the dispositional aspects of emotion wherein a life is shaped over time in the teachings and the actual practice of faith in human relationships. True religion consists in the practical exercises of the will, where the deeper affections are motives and wellsprings of desire and action. Thus Edwards observes that true saints possess a "sense of the heart" as a steady and abiding principle in their lives. They are not simply filled with continuous sensations of piety or commotions of the soul.

This turn in Edwards is decisive for his attempt to understand the religious awakening of his time. It is decisive for our theological attempt at understanding as well. I am not concerned directly, as he was, to identify operations of divine grace as something quite distinct from the capacities of human nature. Nevertheless, Edwards' way of sketching the religious affections provides reliable guidance into the territory I wish to explore.

For Edwards, as with Bernard of Clairvaux, Thomas Aquinas and most post-modern theologians, the very nature of religious affections necessarily involves the intellect. The object of faith is understood and known in and through teachings assimilated by the heart. The appearance of grace in the soul was not simply a new faculty of understanding - as though faith were a world view or an intellectual interpretation of God and the world. Edwards argues that faith is constituted by a new disposition of the heart which orders all the powers of emotion, perception, will, and understanding. The affected heart and the intellect are not opposed in true faith; nor are they finally two different kinds of capacities which are joined by an act of will. In a passage that might well have come from St. Augustine, he says:

> As, on the one hand, there must be light in the understanding, as well as an affected fervent heart, where there is heat without light, there can be nothing divine or heavenly in that heart; so on the other hand, where there is a kind of light without heat, a head stored with notions and speculations, with a cold and unaffected heart, there can be nothing divine in that light, that knowledge is no true spiritual knowledge of divine things.[5]

This passage expresses a point we encounter in the greatest of the patristic and later monastic spiritual writers: knowledge of God is always gained through love and fear of God. "Experience" here does not imply something esoteric or extraordinary. Rather, the realities of faith are understood primarily as "lived faith." Study, prayer, and work, and the concrete life of human relationships are the exercises of this understanding of the heart. St. Benedict speaks of the *affectus,* or grace of prayer, as the manner of savoring the divine teachings.[6] The "objective" knowledge of God was, for the great theologians such as St. Bernard, a preparation for a knowledge by *affectus* — the wisdom of fearing and loving God.

For Edwards the most important and distinguishing aspect of Christian experience lies in the practices of the virtues. The degree of faith, he claims, is to be judged "by the fixedness and strength of the habit that is exercised in affection, whereby holy affection is habitual."[7] In other words, the intentions and actions of the believer must themselves flow from the affective understanding of the relevant doctrines. In this way the affections are not simply interior states of sudden feeling. They are the "more vigorous and sensible exercises of the inclination and will."[8] Only when religious emotions become deep and abiding motives ought we to speak of them as holy affections which are the distinguishing marks of true religious faith.

Struggling to address misunderstandings by the rationalist orthodoxies on the one hand and those of emotionally charged enthusiastic religion on the other, Jonathan Edwards illuminates a pathway for subsequent theological work on the affections. Hence his work provides a touchstone for my explorations concerning religious affections in the context of prayer.

Questions about emotion and the affections are frequently regarded today as psychological rather than properly theological questions. Emotions essential to religious life and particularly to the practice of prayer are commonly categorized as "subjective" in the sense of "private." To many religious people and to many systematic theologians, the affections do not seem the sort of thing susceptible of being clarified by theological reflection. Yet this is precisely my aim — to present a theological investigation of the religious affections. Such deep emotions, which are ingredient in a Christian understanding of God and the world, are more than a matter of the psychology of religious behavior. Nor are they the exclusive subject of ascetical and pastoral theology. They are essential to fundamental theology as well, to the explication of our primary language about God which is embedded in the stories, images, and concepts of Scripture and worship. To understand this primary language involves the unfolding of the religious affections — their role and their logic.

Whatever else it may include, the Christian faith is a pattern of deep emotions.[9] It is gratitude to God for creation and redemption, awe and holy fear of the divine majesty, repentant sorrow over our sins, joy in God's steadfast love and mercy, and love of God and neighbor. To confess faith in God is to live a life characterized by these emotions. The relation between being a Christian and possessing a pattern of such emotions is so intimate that anyone who lacks this particular gratitude, fear, penitence, joy and love, can be said to be Christian in name only. To say that one loves God while dwelling in hatred for one's neighbor is to misunderstand who God is.

Such an intimate relation between religious belief and certain emotions is not, of course, peculiar to Christianity. It belongs quite generally to religious beliefs, as I show in the next chapter. All serious moral and religious ways of life have to do with the acquiring and ordering of deep emotions in the sense I am proposing.[10] Some religious traditions aim at the cessation of all human emotion in the name of a greater good. Within the Christian ascetic tradition there is the call for *apatheia*, a becoming passionless. But in every religious way of life a form of control over the dark passions is found. Such control almost always, even in the ascetic traditions of prayer, involves the acquiring and refinement of other emotions. Thus, love is to drive out fear and hatred, humility is to replace envy and greed, and trust to quell anxiety.

From this angle of vision, to be human is to be capable of a range of emotions. Everyone loves and hates, desires to be happy, and wishes to avoid pain and death. To be human is to be open to joy and sorrow, gladness and hope, gratitude and enmity. In taking up a certain way of life, we come to have such emotions in *particular* ways to learning to value specific attitudes, actions, and persons in life. The emotions are made determinate as the world is perceived in specific ways - as a prison house or a garden of delights, a heartless chaos or a created order. This is natural to all humanity. But to choose a certain moral or religious view of the world and to adopt a way of life congruent with it is to take up a particular set of passions and emotions.

Something more is also involved. In taking up a way of life portrayed and proclaimed in the Christian Scripture, human beings are given a new teacher as well as teachings. The particularity of Christian affections has to do with the objects toward which they are directed. Left to our own devices, we may learn joy or grief or gratitude in relation to a wide range of things. But within the Christian life, we come to have gratitude for our creation, preservation, and redemption in God who brings salvation. One learns to grieve over wrong, and rejoice in mercy and justice. In this way, the grounds for having a particular set of emotions become crucial for theology. The essential feature of the order among Christian emotions is that they take God and the acts of God's as their object and their ground.

We begin to see how emotions are connected with specific teachings about God and the world, a point to which I return in detail in the next two chapters. For now, it is enough to have established the fact that Christianity is, among other things, a set and a particular ordering of emotions.

This still may leave us somewhat puzzled, however. Are not emotions inner, "subjective" feelings? If so, how could we ever determine whether members of a particular religious tradition share the same emotions? Such questions betray a set of misunderstandings. Let us uncover some of these misunderstandings which prevent a clear view of human emotion more generally considered.

Human emotions are still regarded by many philosophers and theologians as peripheral to the task of seeking knowledge and truth about reality. The ordinary person is perhaps no better off. From the pages of Western philosophy and theology we inherit a dominant set of contrasts between reason and passion, thoughts and feeling, judgment and emotion. This has been especially so in modern times, but its roots are very deep in ancient habits of thought. Maturity, both individual and social, has often been pictured as the control of our "lower nature" by reason. The intellect is to rule the passions — so the chief council of common sense has been. Thinkers of considerable stature have conceived reason to be the essence of our humanity, while the passions have been typically regarded as dark and unruly, belonging to our sensible nature. Indeed, the passions have been quite naturally regarded as linking human beings to the animal world. This has led some thinkers to declare that in matters of morals or ethics, human desires, emotions and passions must be avoided.[11]

Thus the traditional views of passions and emotions have generated confusions and misunderstandings of enormous consequence which even today govern our common sense ideas.

The passions have generally been looked upon as violent and disordering features of human life. The notion that our loves and hates, fears and joys are basically disruptive forces in life is a dominant viewpoint especially in twentieth-century psychology. The stability and temperance of reason is contrasted with the torrent and tempest of the passions. If it was difficult in the seventeenth century to think clearly about the passions, it seems more bewildering in the twentieth. So many competing concepts of emotion have arisen. The various field of psychology and the "science" of human behavior, each with its popular counterpart, propose different and often conflicting definitions of emotion and the passions.

This creates a problem, since most of these definitions are still couched in terms of distrust of human subjectivity. In its original sense, "passion" referred to those things which human beings *suffer*. In its classical meaning, the word refers to the state of mind which results from something acting upon us. We are passive in face of the passions. Some passions may be happy, such as love, hope and joy; while others may be painful, such as fear, grief, or anger. Underlying this way of regarding our emotional life is the assumption that we cannot help being overcome by passions, since they are basically responses to forces outside us.

This classical notion of human passions has carried over into many of our modern views of emotion. Our emotional life seems to us, regarded as a whole, to be involuntary and disruptive. We tend to think of "passions" today as the most violent and turbulent of our emotions. But though the term "emotion" has greater usage in everyday language than the older term, it seems almost too vague and obscure. This is in part because we use it to refer to feelings, moods and a wide range of affectivity. Because in our everyday life we continue to talk about emotions in this way, I must clarify the term. My task is to mark differences between emotions, feelings and moods where we ordinarily do not. The misunderstanding of emotions which has been carried over from the earlier concept of the passions must be corrected. The term "affections" is intended to overcome some of these difficulties, even though it may seem too closely associated with mere warm sentiment, or gentle feelings.

Here we do well to follow the lead of Edwards in marking a distinction between passion and affection.

> The affections and passions are frequently spoken of as the same; and yet, in the more common use of speech, there is in some respect a difference; and affection . . .seems to be something more extensive than passion; being used for all vigorous lively actings of the will or inclination; but passion for those that are more sudden, and whose effects on the animal spirits are more violent, and the mind more overpowered, and less in its own command.[12]

In Edwards we still encounter the suggestion that we should distrust the passions. By such a contrast, we point to the more encompassing feature of human emotional life whereby the ups and downs of our everyday life of feeling are given order and a certain tonal center. The relevance of this point is well expressed by Richard R. Niebuhr:

> It is not sufficient to conceive of faithful man in the world as a rational soul, nor even as a rational being whose dignity lies in choosing and willing. He is also an affectional being whose thinking and willing are themselves always qualified by the specific affection or resonance that pervades the whole person world polarity.[13]

The point here is to reject the basic distrust of human subjectivity which we inherit with our common vocabulary of passion and emotion. Such general distrust is, I think rooted in the idea that "being objective" or "rational" is to have rules and standards for life and discourse, while "being objective" or "being affected" is to have none. Indeed, if passions and feelings are inner phenomena in human life over which we have no immediate control, how can we help but oppose these to the rationality of our thoughts, ideas, and judgments about the world? If emotions are simply hidden mental events, or complex sensations happening "within" us (based partly in our physiological makeup), then they are indeed unruly. We habitually regard such inner episodes as "what we feel" caused by events and objects outside us. This way of understanding emotion as inner responses to outer stimulations makes us think that our passions and emotions can only be understood as mysterious happenings within, or external regularities in human behavior. They are rooted in the body, and as such appear to be completely different from thinking, reasoning, evaluating, and making judgments. The latter lead to objectivity, while the emotions seem hopelessly subjective.

Our common sense tendency to regard emotions as inner effects of external events is reinforced by popular psychology. Either emotions are involuntary inner feelings or nothing but regularities in our behavior, as B.F. Skinner and others have argued. Now if my sorrow or joy or love is "inside" me as it appears when I look within, then it is privately my own. If I am overwhelmed by feelings of remorse or of joy, then I alone seem to be the first to know. Any further knowledge of my emotions will, if this view is correct, only come from the inside of the person who feels the emotions. In turn, this view leads to other popular ideas such as "only a woman can know such an emotion," or "only people of the same ethnic group can know how each other feels." Emotions here are understood only by similarity of blood or historical circumstance.

However appealing such views may be, they lead us astray. Lumping all emotional features of life together in opposition to the objective rational powers of the person leads to confusion and untruth. Surely a primary reason why we do not know another's joy or grief or anger, is that we do not believe or recognize or think certain things which the other person believes, recognizes or thinks. Perhaps we have chosen not to, or perhaps we live in innocent ignorance. We therefore do not regard the objects of joy or grief or anger in the same way. It is not, as we shall discover in the next chapter, that the language of emotions is private or hopelessly parochial or inadequate. Rather, sharing the same regard or appraisal of things is necessary to share in the same emotions. We must know a wide range of life as "shameful," "joyful," "dangerous," or "lovely" in order to be capable of those emotions. We cannot, of course, divorce such knowings and judgments from the social histories of persons and institutions. But even though circumstances which cause similar patterns of emotion in people are "social products," the having of distinct emotions still has its own structure and dynamic. What it is to *have* an emotion can never fully be explained by describing what *causes* it.

As Paul Holmer has observed,

> One cannot grieve over the fate of his country unless he has learned to love it, so, too, one must have loved deeply to feel the poignancy of betrayal. However, to say all of that is to admit that emotions are conditional, but conditional upon all the facts that make for a significant evaluation and description . . .of a state of affairs, of human behavior, or of the way life now is.[14]

In light of such basic consideration, we need to revise many of our inherited ideas about emotions and about being "subjective." The distrust of subjectivity which philosophers and theologians often show will not help us either. We cannot, of course, deny that our emotional lives are often chaotic and unruly. We should not deny that we are overcome or disturbed or rendered incapable of clear thought on many occasions. It is quite appropriate in certain circumstances to say that we cannot help how we feel. We do in fact learn to "control" intense feelings of various emotions such as anger, fright, anxiety, and the like.

All this ought to alert us to the *difference* between having an emotion and feeling particular sensations, say, at the onset of a particular emotion. Being angry and feeling angry are different in many cases, just as being thankful and feeling thankful may be. This in itself shows that emotions cannot be "merely subjective." Emotions are never uncontrollable inner happenings as such. Undergoing or experiencing our emotions is only one aspect of having emotions.

Inherited common sense ideas about passion and emotion ignore the fact that the learning of emotions and passions is accessible only through descriptions of the world, real or imagined. Great literature and the books of Scripture portray possibilities for our emotional life. One of the most common ways of learning and expressing emotions is in and through language. The most notable case is poetry; and it is no accident that much of Scripture contains poetry or at least uses the poetic powers of language to describe persons, events, and the experience of God.

Emotions, like thoughts, can be either vague or precise. The more deeply an emotion is "lived into," the more it involves understanding the specific objects toward which the emotion is directed, and the specific occasion which prompts the emotion. Again the function of literature and poetry, and much of Scripture as well, is to arouse, sustain, and articulate deep emotions, not by "causing" certain subjective feelings, but by offering evaluative images and descriptions of reality. Because metaphors, images, and symbols are involved, we speak of the power of the imagination in such language to engage the self. To live with and to understand something by a deep metaphor or image — for example, that of "the face of God" — requires understanding in and through affectional regard.

The principal point is that in the moral and religious life, we are more accountable for what we *are* than for what we immediately feel. This signals a contrast between our emotions and our immediate feelings. We will explore the connection between emotion and motive in the pages which follow, preserving something of the older notion of emotions and affections as "motions of the soul." What we *are* in our intentions and actions, is more adequately revealed by referring to the dispositions which constitute a "sense" of the heart than by referring to what we feel or what ideas we have at the time. To say that a person has a deep sense of gratitude is to remark upon his or her character. To understand that emotion in its depth, we must see what is true of that individual in various situations year upon year. The evidence of such gratitude will be found in his or her actions, perceptions, and feelings. Such a deep sense is what we shall call an emotion or an affection. It is not a feeling as such since it cannot be an episodic event "inside" the person. Neither can it be a mood because it involves distinguishing those things for which one is grateful from those over which one must be sorrowful or indignant. Moods do not require such mental capacities. Rather, a deep sense of gratitude is a disposition.

Such emotions, when found in the context of teachings about God, are the religious affections in this "dispositional" sense, rather than complex sensations, feelings, or moods. Christian thankfulness, repentance, and compassion are dispositions to act, to perceive, and to feel which characteristically dwell at the center of a personal life in the "heart." They are given their particular character by virtue of the stories, concepts, and practices which belong to Christianity.

Finally, we must learn to distinguish shallow and deep emotions. This is part of human moral maturity. Moreover, such distinctions are essential to any understanding of the life of prayer and religious experience. No doubt there can be pompous, trivial, or vulgar exercises of religious piety, just as our lives can be pompous, vulgar, or trivial quite apart from religious teachings and practices. As Jonathan Edwards saw so clearly, having a great deal of "feeling of elation" or behaving in grossly emotional ways may in fact betray a certain shallowness, or even desperation. It may also lead to the self-deception of feigning deeper faith than one possesses.

Such a distinction between shallowness and depth with respect to the emotions is not achieved theoretically. It is, in the full sense of the word, "existential." This contrast can only be gained by existing a certain way. We must reflect upon specific ways in which our lives are refined and modified by particular teachings and practices. Part of the power in the concept of the religious affections lies in the extent of human behavior governed by such emotional capacities. The connection between beliefs about God and the emotional capacities formed in those who pray shows a definite shape. I have called this a "grammar" of faith. Where the teachings of Scripture are fully understood, they require the learning of certain enduring emotions. "The fear of the Lord is the beginning of wisdom." To believe that God redeems, judges, and shows compassion for the contrite, involves a distinctive set of affections. Without such a particular subjectivity, the concepts and teachings about God cannot be fully grasped in their religious sense.

There is no religious life without our being profoundly affected: doctrine without experience is empty; religious experience without doctrine is blind. Just because this is so, we need to begin where Edwards began, by setting forth the centrality and the necessity of the religious affections as a key to understanding what prayer is. Only this way can both doctrine and life be understood in their proper relations to prayer as the paraphrase of the soul.

two

Prayer as the Language of the Heart

Miguel De Unamuno, in his *Tragic Sense of Life*, expresses vividly the connection between belief in God and the language of emotion:

> Those who say that they believe in God and yet neither love nor fear Him, do not in fact believe in Him, but in those who have taught them that God exists . . .Those who believe that they believe in God, but without any passion in their heart, without anguish of mind, without uncertainty, without doubt, without an element of despair even in their consolation, believe only in the God-Idea, not in God.[1]

The language of religious faith is the language of emotion. This much is a commonplace. Among believers it is often said that the language of faith is the "language of the heart." This is no accident; for surely one of the most basic metaphors in Scripture and in religious literature is the human heart. By it, biblical faith refers to the very essence of a human being, to the inmost center of personal existence.

When religious faith speaks in prayer and worship, we often say that its language gives expression to the deepest aspirations, hopes, desires, and experiences of the human heart.

My heart overflows with a goodly theme.

Create in me a clean heart, O God.

Our hearts are restless until they find rest in Thee.

17

The emotions, attitudes, and feelings which are part of the structure of religious beliefs are found in such language: praise, sorrow, contrition, anguish, hope, and joy. There is nothing so obvious, yet so difficult to make clear to the skeptic.

My aim in this chapter is to understand anew the full significance of why we call the language of prayer and worship the language of the heart. Consider the expression, "to feel something deeply in one's heart." We use it frequently. It is not in itself a religious utterance since it can be said about nearly anything. It is related to other expressions we often use, "Take it to heart" and "I mean this with all my heart." These are signs of seriousness. Yet such expressions are subject to much abuse as well. In our time, they have become the signal of mere sentimentality - covering remarks for vague and only half-formed thoughts and feelings. We should be wary if we do not know the speaker well enough to know what surrounds and keeps company with these expressions in that persons's life. It is simply a fact that many people abuse the language of the heart and thereby deaden the metaphor.

Still, these can be revelatory remarks, indicating matters of passionate conviction and commitment. Such utterances are kin to human endeavors which are "whole-hearted." They invite considerations which go to the core of our humanity - to our capacities of feeling and intending life at full strength. If the concept of the human heart, metaphorical as it is, has fallen into disrepute, that is to our impoverishment. For we need such a concept in order to refer to the matrix of human passions and thought. Above all, matters of the heart are not simply for people who do not wish to think or make judgments in life. The concept of the heart both explains and governs our lives.[2]

The concept of the heart and its language is indispensable to common life, even though it lies open to trivialization. This is because it is not a technical term belonging to a particular human science, or to a specialized domain of learning. The glory of the concept and its related expressions is that we learn to use it without benefit of technical education. It is on our lips because we have need to say things about ourselves and our existence which requires a concept of the "center" of our thoughts, emotions, and active behavior. An account of the ways in which we human beings live and move and have our being must eventually reckon with the language of the heart in one or more of its moral and religious forms.

In the first chapter I pointed out that, in literature, language works to engender and even to create emotions. In much of the classical tradition of the novel, for example, we learn of the human heart this way. Human emotions are portrayed through the narrative of character and life, and are not simply stimulated by a frontal assault, much less by naming and defining them. We learn the ways of the human heart by descriptions of how persons live in the world - their behavior, motives, thoughts, and passions.

So it is that the most central questions concerning life and death, love and hatred, or good and evil, require that we speak of these concerns in relation to how we are affected in the stream of our days. This is why matters of morals and religion seem to the objective philosophical or scientific mind to be "subjective" - precisely because they involve determinations in one's emotional life as well as in one's mind. To speak or to resolve "with all one's heart" is therefore much richer and more concrete than making up our minds according to "the principles of objective reason."

There are indeed reasons of the heart which are far more than sentimental urges or intuitions based upon moods. Dostoievsky foresaw with dread an emerging culture in which affections of the heart and conscience would meet with denial, or become meaningless in a kind of general cynicism - the despair of a "loveless" mechanical society. In such a society, he observed, there would be neither tragedy, nor moral sensibility, nor faith.

To characterize the "heart of man" is thus to sketch the shape of particular lives. To say that the heart is fearful, enraged, despairing, joyful, courageous, or grateful is to say that human beings are alive and motivated or driven in these ways. Even more, to know the heart is to discern the way in which the world is received, and to ask whether things in the world are truthfully perceived to be what they are. In this sense too, the language of the heart is not reducible to private subjective concerns. Our knowledge of the human passions and motives, and our ways of being deeply affected are related to how we know the world and choose to dwell therein. To take up the language of the heart is to have access to moral and religious valuations of the world.

Yet to know the heart of another is also to learn the ambiguities of that individual's loves, fears and joys. In this way we come to learn of our own passions and emotions as well, not because we share some metaphysically invariable entity called the heart, but because we share in the human race by virtue of our capacity for emotions and passions, vices and virtues. As Kierkegaard observed, "at every moment the individual is himself and the race." "Every individual is essentially interested in the history of all other individuals . . . While the history of the race goes on, the individual regularly begins afresh, because he is himself and the race, and hence in turn his is the history of the race."[3] To know the heart of another human being is to know the legacy of the society to which that person belongs.

This is also why knowledge of the human heart is much more complex than knowledge about the human mind. Ambiguities of the heart run through all thoughts and projects fashioned in light of human passions. Because we cannot achieve the same kind of agreement and universality about emotions as we can about ideas or theories, it may seem that knowledge of the human heart is less significant than knowledge of the intellect. But surely this is not so, for there can be agreement in matters of the heart. A shared passion for truth and hatred of ignorance binds persons together in mutual knowledge. Such agreements in the judgments and reasons of the heart are obviously complex and difficult; but this is because they are of such import, not because they belong to the "subjective" realm of emotions and beliefs.

It should be clear, then, why the Scriptures appeal so frequently to the metaphor of the heart, and why this language is present at every turn. Consider some familiar instances: "for the Lord sees not as man sees; man looks on the outward appearance, but the Lord looks on the heart" (I Samuel16:7); "you shall love the Lord your God with all your heart, and with all your soul, and with all your might" (Deuteronomy 6:5); "you have become obedience from the heart" (Romans 6:17); "Mary kept all these things, pondering them in her heart: (Luke 2:19). Our point is not to proof-text, but to show how clearly the focus of the metaphor is upon that which is most worthy and deepest in human beings. The "heart" is a place of conscience and moral capacity. In and through all the Old and New Testament literature there runs the theme that God looks upon and judges the heart and is not deceived. That is why God can be said to be "greater than our hearts."

The concept of the heart, then, is strangely authoritative in Scripture because it gathers to a focal point a whole range of ordinary ways in which human beings explain themselves to each other. We understand ourselves as members of the human race and make ourselves clear to one another by describing and explaining our fears, hopes, loves, joys - in short, our intentions and motives. The human race being what it is, there are no general psychological or sociological laws and behavioral theories which comprehend the richness and authority of these more ordinary ways of describing and explaining our lives. So "the heart" not only explains what we do, it governs who we are.

We are not saying that there is some standard way the heart must be, as though underlying all human passions was some universal tendency. The heart must learn, so to speak, what it is to be. Thus different views of life form and shape the center of human life differently. This is why the matter of judging who among us are courageous, contrite, faithful, dishonest, or glad involves learned capacities. Some things about persons and the world are known only by virtue of having already gained certain emotions.

Now we turn to a more detailed consideration of how emotion and belief are interrelated in prayer conceived as the "language of the heart." Some who have thought hard about the relation between theology and the language of prayer have argued that all theological statements are disguised expressions of emotion, attitude, and feeling. It is not merely that prayer expresses emotion, but that all language about God is nothing more than the expression of human sentiment masquerading under the form of statements about God and the world. In short, these philosophers wish to reduce theology to "emotive" language. But this is a mistaken theory of monumental proportions. It fails to see that in matters of religion (and morals as well) the having of certain emotions is part of what it means to hold certain beliefs.

Though we may avoid the brash conclusion that all theology is nothing but "feeling" made objective, the language of worship and prayer may still strike us as being subjective. This parallels the idea that the human heart is, after all, a dispensable metaphor. If we conceive of prayer and worship as the language of the heart, what is to prevent us from drawing a sharp line between the poetic, expressive language of prayer, and the objective, "truth-bearing language of theology?" In order to avoid such a misunderstanding, we need to show how the language of prayer and worship is the language of emotion.

There are many circumstances in which we need to call attention to the difference between how things are and how we feel about them. Sometimes what we believe and how we feel are deliberately separated. Think, for example, of: "I believe taxes are too high, but that doesn't bother me"; or "I believe there will always be corruption in society, but it doesn't matter." Other people will, of course, feel differently. More generally, however, modernity teaches us to think that how we feel doesn't have anything to do with the "facts." Because in many aspects of our life we in fact separate what is so from how we feel about it, we tend to generalize this to cover all cases. The contrast between what we believe and the emotions we have toward that particular matter tends to become a dichotomy. A commonsense view of life often includes the assumption that this general distinction holds with respect to all human language. Beliefs are one kind of thing, while emotions are another, even though we may admit that somehow both go on "in the mind." If we approach the language of prayer with this assumption, we will never understand the sense in which praying to God forms and expresses matters of the "heart."

Suppose someone says that he believes that handguns are quite dangerous, but that he does not fear them. He may pick one up and appear quite calm. This seems reasonable, though we certainly expect him to treat the gun carefully. This is a relatively clear case of the separability of belief from emotion. Suppose, however, that another person claims that all mad dogs are vicious, yet says he never fears them, If he yawns and dozes off when one actually appears, we begin to detect an oddness about his "belief." Either he is extremely "fearless" by nature, or he may be very clever at masking or controlling his fear. Or, he might not really believe that mad dogs are frightening in the way his initial remark seemed to imply. In this case we expect the show of certain emotions and feelings to be evidence of his belief that mad dogs are dangerous.

Allow me one more simple case: A woman believes that the bonfire will burn her. She is afraid of the fire. When she says she is afraid at breakfast, she is not just reporting something she feels. She is in fact expressing her belief. We can certainly imagine her in the midst of a burning building being overwhelmed by her feelings of fear. But the emotion of fear in this case is not simply what she feels at such a particular moment, it is a pervasive feature of her life. In fact her fearing the effects of the fire is inseparable from what she believes about fires.[4] This shows again, as noted earlier, that we do learn to distinguish having an emotion from feeling the emotion in a particular circumstance.

If this is true in examples drawn from the language of everyday life, how much more it may be true of the language of religious faith. My point here is that, in certain instances in the language of prayer, emotion and belief as intrinsically related. It is not that I am doing away with the contrast between what we feel and what we believe. Rather, I seek to clarify the conceptual relation between specific beliefs and emotions in the language of prayer and worship. Can we claim that the language of prayer gives expression to emotions in language which necessarily describes what is believed about God and the believer's relation to God?

Some familiar language from the Psalms provides a useful reminder:

Have mercy on me, O God, according to thy steadfast love; according to thy abundant mercy blot out my transgressions. (Psalm 51:1)

I give thee thanks, O Lord with my whole heart; before the gods, I sing thy praise;...and give thanks to thy name for thy steadfast love and thy faithfulness. (Psalm 138:1-2)

As a hart longs for flowing streams, so longs my soul for thee, O God. (Psalm 42:1)

What interests us here is the manner in which descriptions and ascriptions of God are intrinsic features of the language as repentance, desire, praise, and longing. These are not untypical cases of the language of prayer. Time and again, the emotion of the believer - sorrow over sin, gratitude and joy in God, and the like - is made clear in and through language which attributes certain things to God. Learning this language is like learning both the emotions and beliefs in their correlation. In the case of the Psalms, those who pray these texts are not necessarily "feeling" their emotions spontaneously; but the praying requires, in some, an entering into the language, and a disposition toward the specific belief-laden emotions which are presented in the prayer.

The classical collect form of prayer shows this tie-up between emotions and belief very clearly. The petition is always dependent upon the particular characteristic or attribute of God that is singled out in the opening ascription:

Almighty God, unto whom all hearts are open, all desires known, and from whom no secrets are hid: Cleanse the thoughts of our hearts by the inspiration of thy Holy Spirit, that we may perfectly love thee, and worthily magnify thy holy Name, through Christ our Lord.[5]

In addressing God as the one who knows the heart and thus the whole of our lives, we make clear what is believed in the very asking for purity of heart. Coming in humility to stand open for God's forgiving and strengthening Spirit, those who pray also manifest what is believed about God. Indeed, this particular prayer contains an extraordinary amount of theology compressed into a single utterance. The intention to love and praise God with one's whole heart and mind is compacted into the petition and its consequence. This is a momentous asking, indeed. It indicates a readiness to enter into the very divine life itself; or rather, to have the very life of God dwell in the believer.

From these few examples, we note that the language of prayer - in this liturgical prayer - evokes and educates us in certain specific emotions by ascribing to God what is believed about God in the vocative mode. Thus in coming to regard God in certain affective patterns, our own personal existence is involved. Religious beliefs require our having certain affections formed in the language: by describing something with metaphor and image. We are not merely referring to or naming emotions or inner feelings. Quite the contrary, our attention and affective intention targets God and, in so doing, it involves those deeper dimensions of the human self expressed in the metaphor of the heart.

The language of prayer not only "expresses" emotion in these ways, it forms and critiques the emotional life as well. This point is often neglected in accounts of the relationship between prayer and religious experience. If we ask how the language of prayer and worship form and refine our emotions, an adequate answer would begin to encompass the inner logic or grammar of the Christian life itself. This book is one such beginning. In the remainder of this chapter, we turn to an examination of the relation between belief and emotion in the specific case of sorrow and remorse over one's sin before God.

Such emotions as are articulated in Psalms and liturgical prayers of the Church are dependent upon believing specific things about God. These emotions are linked to descriptions of self and the world as well. They are not merely stimulated by the language as inchoate feeling-states. In most examples, the thought that we are sinners before God is the occasion for the appropriate emotions such as regret, remorse or sorrow. Depending upon what situation in life we are concerned to highlight, we may say that the having of such emotions is an exercise of the belief that we are sinful; or that praying with penitent hearts brings one to attend to God in and through the emotions belonging to repentance.

But there is something peculiar about the "object" of such religious emotions which must be faced. It may seem that we must have independent ways of describing the object of the emotions if we are to escape the problem of error or self-deception. To put it bluntly, can we be wrong about remorse and sorrow over sin?

In order to get a clearer idea of the issue, consider a non-religious example. We say of someone that he suffers remorse because he broke his promise. Remorse involves the belief that one has done something wrong and knows it. Normally we mark a difference between someone who is remorseful because an actual wrong was committed and someone who is remorseful because he only thinks or believes that a wrong has been done. If we find out that no wrong has in fact been done, we can alter or remove the sorrow and remorse by correction of what is now a false belief. In describing the true situation we can change his emotion, provided our description is accepted.

Of course in both these cases, a person's feeling remorse requires a belief that a wrong has been done. The fact that one could be mistaken does not take away this logical connection. We are also familiar with situations in which a person may know that he broke a promise, for example, and yet experiences no remorse at all. Other factors intrude, such as his own weariness of breaking the promises to the point of cynicism or moral defeat. Or, he may have what is a justifying reason for having broken a promise in this particular occasion. For example, "Yes, I admit I broke the promise, but I did it to save him." But in general we agree that a promise-breaker who suffers no remorse whatever suffers from a defect in character. We may attribute the lack of an emotion to a moral flaw in the person. In serious cases we might say that a person who lacks a capacity for remorse is incapable of feeling sorrow over his own wrongdoing. This is akin to having no "sense" of sin.

Yet in the case of religious emotions there is an added factor. While a certain familiar pattern of experience from everyday life clusters around guilt, remorse, and sorrow and part of our praying, the concept of sin decisively relates these experiences to God's holiness and righteousness. In the traditional "Prayer of General Confession" or in the "Act of Contrition," we speak of being "heartily sorry for these our misdoings, the remembrance of them is grievous unto us." This particular grieving is dependent upon having understood the concept of God as holy. The occasion around such feelings may be a parable or a reading or a sermon which recalls wrongdoing in one's life. The object of such emotions is not simply the thought or the remembrance, however. Rather, sorrow is part of the judgment one renders on oneself. "Sin before God" is the complex object of this emotion. This itself is a self-description arising out of religious stories and beliefs concerning the relationship between human beings and God. Hence, the following peculiarity.

Ordinarily we can correct feeling remorse on false grounds because we can get at the matter of whether one did in fact break a promise - to use our previous example. But in the case of remorse over one's sinfulness, we cannot get at the cause independently of the concept of "sin before God." In coming to use the language of sin and repentance, we learn that there can be no mistake about our being sinful, though we certainly can be mistaken about a specific sinful act. The very notion of sin is such that it guarantees the object toward which the emotions of sorrow and remorse are directed. Of course, a person can always use the language without "meaning" it. But this is a different point about the truthfulness of the utterance, not about the object of these emotions.

Religious beliefs are not only a necessary part of the occasion of such emotions: the belief that one is a sinner before God is also a reason for experiencing the emotions of sorrow and remorse. The act of confessing one's sins in corporate prayer is a special context in which the belief is rehearsed in the language of the community. Such a context of penitential prayer forms personal capacities for self-judgment in light of one's relationship to God. The particular kinds of feelings experienced in confessing may vary considerably from time to time and from individual to individual. These accompanying feelings of sorrow and remorse, and their intensity of affective tone cannot and should not be denied. They are related to the act of saying just these particular words of the prayer and meaning them. Meaning what is said in confessing one's sin requires that the capacity for sorrow or remorse be exercised. This does not, however, involve undergoing or "experiencing" feelings in a particular standard way in order to have confessed truly.

If we apply the terms *emotion* or *affection* in prayer and worship only to the temporary episodes of feeling "inside" the person, we miss an essential feature of religious affections. They are conceptually dependent upon beliefs and upon the capacity to judge oneself in light of particular stories and descriptions of the world. The language of prayer cannot, in this sense, be purely expressive of inner experiences. It is surely true that *in praying*, all manner of intense experience, including inchoate feelings may arise. These may accompany the exercise of our capacity for remorse, but are not necessary for being sorry for our sins. It is more important that such prayers result in living one's life more intensely.

Earlier I referred to a woman's belief and fear that the fire will burn. There is a strong anology here with persons believing themselves sinners before a forgiving God, and their being penitent. Whatever inner episodes of feeling may occur, such sensations are not the kind of phenomena which can constitute the regulative expression of those specific beliefs. The disposition to feel a certain way is part of having an emotion. But the connection between a particular belief about God and that particular emotion does not depend upon a specific way of feeling the emotion. Yet it is important that one be affected in admitting one's sins before God. As the classical prayer of confession from the Anglican Prayer Book states of wrong-doings, "the remembrance of them is grievous unto us." The penitent is "heartily sorry," though not always and equally in the same way.

Now if someone asks: "what determines whether one truly believes oneself to be a sinner?" then appeals to certain experiences in one's life may well be in order. Persons who never felt remorse, sorrow or grief over sin may not believe, but only think they do. On the other hand, a person who continuously massages the feeling of remorse and constantly needs to "feel sorry" may never have truly repented.

We may say, then, that in the language of prayer, beliefs about ourselves before God are held in the manner of affections. It is tempting to say that the beliefs are the emotions. At least we should say that the believing is the exercise of the emotion in rehearsing life before God in prayer. Since believing is not something we do in episodes, neither is the having of the appropriate emotions something confined to the episodic "experiencing" of the emotion. In the foregoing analysis my point was to show that unless the confession of sin is part of a much larger pattern of self-judgment and relocation of desire, it simply is not adequate to what we mean by confessing one's sins before God.

But note the implications. Sometimes the teaching about sinfulness occasions the emotion which leads one to grow into the belief that one has trespassed against another. But we may also understand that we do in fact so believe by reflecting upon the intensity of our sorrow and remorse over wrongdoing. We think immediately of St. Paul's anguished remark: "For I do not do the good I want, but the evil I do not want is what I do."[6] This is not, however, just any "natural" sorrow and remorse. It is conceptually related to stories about God and human sin. Coming to mean what one says in prayer and worship is intimately related to the education of our capacities for sorrow and remorse. What makes the latter distinctive is the way they are specified by religious teachings.

Prayer, then, is the rule-keeping activity of the language of the heart. It is not just a matter of keeping a certain way of talking alive; it is a way of keeping certain religious emotions in place. To demand, however, that prayer require a distinctive set of inner experiences of feeling-states would be to misunderstand the internal relations between religious beliefs and emotions.

What we think and believe about God, the world, and human life is embedded in this language. It arises from the narrative of Scripture and the teachings of tradition in metaphors and images as well as in concepts. Yet it is the language of the heart, not merely of the mind or of the subjective private feelings of individuals.

Theologians have often talked as though a set of beliefs constitute a way of interpretation. Religious beliefs do more than provide a system for "interpreting" the world and our experience. The activity of rehearsing such beliefs in prayer are taken into the very life of the believers. Occasioning the emotions of remorse and sorrow for one's sinfulness for example, forms the person's very character, giving that person the capacity to be a self and to intend the world in specific ways. The activity of praying in which beliefs and emotions are fused in the heart ties together what is spoken about the world consistently with the correction of that human being's own life. Such self-involving criticism of life, with its consequent intention and behavior, is far deeper than a coherent system of thoughts or of statable beliefs.

In religious emotions such as we have described, one's thinking and intending are more than accidentally or causually related to how one's emotions are shaped, and to what one feels deeply. Rather, the relation here is one of coinherence in the person. Having religious emotions in confessing what one is before God who forgives and searches the heart is a necessary part of believing in that God. This is also a matter of fear and trembling. Because such emotions run deeply and pervasively into the heart of personal existence, they form an affective attunement to the whole of one's experience as well. The pattern among religious affections and the web of experience they configure will be the concern of chapter four.

For now we may observe that the language of the heart is not an ornamentation of the language of faith, but its essence. To believe in God is to fear and love and rejoice in God.

Learning to pray is opening oneself to a new way of being; to be formed in a language which shapes and expresses the deep emotions for which we are never quite prepared, and which we would never sustain by our own powers. And, as we shall discover in the next chapter, "meaning" what we pray is linked with entering into the way of life such belief-laden affections call forth. Otherwise, we would believe only in the God-Idea, not in God.

three
Prayer: Shaping and Expressing Emotion

Prayer is dialogue and communion with God, an exploration into the life of God with us. It is therefore a way of intending the world. This way of *intending* the world and its constitutive dispositions, we call prayer: it is both a human activity and a gift, a way of being and of "letting be," an expressing and a being formed. Above all it is a matter of the human heart, in the deepest biblical sense of that metaphor. The hardened heart does not pray, the broken heart cries its prayer, the heart aflame is impassioned toward God. The call to pray and the command to love God with heart, mind, soul, and strength requires the emotional range of fire and water, the freedom of the wind, and the humility of earth.

Having explored some common misunderstandings, and proposed an approach to emotion and belief in the language of faith, I now wish to reflect more fully on prayer and emotion. My thesis is that prayer in all its forms, particularly in its communal forms, both shapes and expresses persons in fundamental emotions. It shapes and gives utterance to the Christian affections, and in so doing provides us with emotional capacities whereby the world may be perceived as God's. Any adequate account of the meaning and point of Christian prayer must clarify both the shaping and the expressing.

I turn first, to specific emotion patterns in communal prayer. Worship is something Christians do together, not just from religious duty (though this may be a sociological fact), but because it is the primary mode of remembering and expressing the Christian faith and the Christian story. In the very activity of re-presenting and rehearsing features of existence described in the story of the Scriptures, worshippers articulate their funda-

29

mental relations to one another and to the world. Worship is in this respect normative. At the same time, not all who participate in its language and action are shaped by it. Not all who say the words of corporate prayer and participate in the ritual prayer actions fully understand what it is to say and do these things. Faith is related to "understanding," but only insofar as it becomes centered in the believing heart. The mere mouthing of the words or the outward observance of the acts of prayer does not unite understanding and the affections.

In corporate worship, Christians engage in language and actions which articulate and shape how they are to be disposed toward the world. Those who say they love God but who are *not* disposed to love and serve the neighbor fail to understand the point of worship in the name of a loving God. In I John we read that anyone who says he loves God and hates his brother is a liar. That seems to me to be a conceptual remark and not an empirical observation about what Christians may or may not do most of the time. It links saying, doing, and understanding in worship with a way of life. To speak of God and to address God in the vocative of prayer means to undertake a certain way of existing, and to behave in a certain way toward other persons. It is easy to overlook this link between learning to address God in worship and becoming disposed toward the world and toward other human beings "in God's name." It is the link between prayer and ethics.

Regarded from a human point of view, prayer is the activity in which human beings explore their life "unto God." It is much more than words. In uttering the words of prayer, we are both doing and "not doing" something. To thank God, to offer praise, to confess, to intercede - all these are ways of giving the self in and through words. What is done with the words is part of the meaning of what is said. Unless we grasp the point of saying such things to God and about God, we will not have fully grasped the language of Scripture and theology in its essentials. Let us recall briefly then, something of the primary emotion range of common prayer.

Prayer is first and last praising, giving thanks, and blessing God. The activity, the gesture of prayer, is utterly naive and utterly vulnerable. It is speaking God's name in gratitude and thankfulness for who God is, and for the world given to us. Classical Jewish prayers always begin, "Blessed are Thou, O Lord our God, King of the Universe." The great Christian prayers of thanksgiving and eucharist often show this same pattern. If someone gives another person a totally unexpected gift - fitted well to that person's interests and delight - the primordial response is a gesture of gratitude, a "thank you." Unless, of course, the world has made us fear that everything has a string attached to it, this form of thanksgiving is fitting to the reception of life as a gift.

It is also essential to our humanity. Prayer is first and last speaking God's name in thanks and praise, and the capacity for gratitude it engenders is required for full humanity. Worship is training in naming God and thereby keeping one essential aspect of the concept of the divine life in place: God is the giver of life and world.

But prayer is also recalling and retelling in awe and adoration. Prayer in corporate worship recalls who and what God is and has done. Huub Oosterhuis has remarked:

> When the Bible prays, the whole of creation is listed and the whole of God's history with man is brought up again. When we pray, with the Bible, we appeal to creation and to the covenant. We call God to mind and remind him who he is and what he has done. What God used to mean for men in the past includes a promise of the future, the promise of the future, the promise that he will mean something for us as well, that he will be someone for us.[1]

So prayer is praise and thanksgiving: the blessing of God for who God is. But secondly, prayer is a recalling and representing - an *anamnesis* - of the story of God in relation to world and humankind; it is memory deepening in awe and adoration. Such vital remembrance is also a crucial part of thanksgiving.

Thirdly, prayer is acknowledgment of who we are in God's sight. For to address God and *mean* what we say, is to recognize our status. Praying thus explores and continually reveals the difference between who God is and what we are in God's sight. We are to be continually shaped by the language of Isaiah in the temple: "Holy, holy, holy . . ." and "Woe is me, for I am a man of unclean lips" (Isaiah 6). But confessing and acknowledging our unworthiness before God also is fitting to certain indelibly human features of our life. If praising and thanking are essential to our full humanity, so is confession. There is a correlation between the attributes of God's holiness and righteousness and our own lack thereof. Prayer enables us to discern and express who and what we are when we are in the presence of God. Confession is part of gaining self-knowledge and truth in the heart.

Finally, though not exhaustively, prayer is intercession. It requires looking clearly and truthfully at the world as it is, being aware of suffering and of the theater of conflicting passions. In interceding for the world and for others, we identify with others and enter into the capacity to bear their burdens. At the very least, this aspect of prayer creates the disposition to pity and compassion toward others. Prayer thus covers the entire range of circumstances and events, good and evil. Prayer as a corporate act of intercession holds the world in all its actuality up to God. In this sense it is a "worldly" activity. It is strenuous because it brings us to truthful perception of the world and of ourselves. Genuine intercessory prayer arouses and sustains the affective kinship with all who suffer. In it we are profoundly affected by the sense of solidarity with the whole race.

In his charming autobiography, *Surprised by Joy,* C.S. Lewis tells of one of the difficulties which contributed to his youthful rejection of the Christian faith. He had been taught that he must not merely "say" his devotions, but must really *mean* what he was uttering. In order really to pray, he was to think about and concentrate upon the words. Of course difficulties ensued. Had he properly meant what he was saying? Was he as intent one time as he had been at another? Not surprisingly, doubts began to undermine his praying, for it seems he was forever falling short of some hopelessly vague ideal. He proposed a solution:

> I set myself a standard. No clause of my prayer was to be allowed to pass muster unless it was accompanied by what I called a 'realization,' by which I meant a certain vividness of the imagination and the affections. My nightly talk was to produce by sheer will power a phenomenon which will power could never produce, which was so ill-defined that I could never say with absolute confidence whether it had occurred, and which, even when it did occur, was of very mediocre spiritual value.[2]

Though his proposed solution was certainly no way out, the young Lewis was struggling with a problem many people face today. This problem involves the connection between "meaning" and the emotions which are referred to and articulated by the prayer texts, whether liturgical or spontaneous. Luther was surely right to remind us, "Where there is true prayer there must be earnestness."[3]

The Pauline text most relevant to these explorations is: "Rejoice always, pray constantly, give thanks in all circumstances; for this is the will of God in Christ Jesus for you" (I Thessalonians 5:16-18). This saying follows a series of reminders on what constitutes living a Christian way of life. Evil and revenge are to be put away; mutual respect and love are to shape one's whole life. In this context St. Paul links praying constantly with living a certain way of life in common. The text, therefore, contains much of what I want to say about emotion and "meaning" in prayer.

Prayer is natural to a life of gratitude. It is not that prayer causes us constantly to feel grateful; rather, the heart who manifests a disposition and sense of gratitude in all its ways. Only in that way of existing does one understand fully why God is to be thanked and praised.[4] The constancy of prayer has to do with the whole of that life oriented toward the constancy of God as the addressee of prayer. Thus St. Paul can command an emotion: "Rejoice!" This reminds those whoi pray of the life they have been given; it is not a call to conjure up objectless inner feelings of elation. Here we begin to see how "meaning" the words is related to a way of intending to live the whole of life. Meaning what one prays belongs to a complex form of life and not simply to episodes of mental effort or sensation.

While prayer should not be regarded exclusively as instruction or as edification, there is one clear sense in which to pray sincerely is to engage in practices which instruct the heart in the knowledge of God. St. Augustine speaks of this sense in *De Sermone in Monte* in which we may see both the logic and the psychology of such instruction.

> But again it can be asked . . .what need there is for this prayer if God already knows what is necessary for us; and the reason can only be that the very effort of prayer calms and purifies our heart and makes it more capable of receiving the divine gifts which are poured out on us spiritually. For God does not hear us out of a desire of receiving our prayers, for he is always ready to give us his light, a light that is not visible, but spiritual and intelligible. We, however, are not always ready to receive it, because we are inclined toward other things and in darkness through our desire for temporary things. In prayer, therefore, there occurs a turning of the heart toward him who is always ready to give if we will only accept what he gives. And in that very turning there is a purifying of the inner eye, since those things which we desire in this world are excluded so that the vision of the single heart can bear the pure light shining from above without any setting or change - and not only bear it but even remain in it, not merely without annoyance but even with the ineffable joy by which a blessed life is truly and genuinely perfected.[5]

Prayer is giving oneself over to God who is ready to give gifts, and to the Christian story in such a way as to rejoice always, to give thanks in all circumstances. The constancy of praying is connected to the manner of living out the emotions required by the Christian life. More clearly perhaps, the praying is logically linked to the emotional capacities: men and women are to live in joy, in gratitude, in mercy, and humility, in love toward each other and toward God. All these things are not just practical aids to prayer, but are an integral part of the life of prayer.

In this sense to mean what one prays is not, as Lewis came to see, to have intense emotional experiences or even to have exquisite powers of imagination. Rather, it is to live in such a way that one's shared form of life is constituted by the characteristics of the subject and object of prayer. This is what Edwards meant in speaking of "practical exercise" of the religious affections.

St. Cyprian, Bishop of Carthage, in his gemlike third-century tract on the Lord's Prayer, reminds his readers of this connection between *praying* and *being*: "If we call God Father, we should behave as His children." Cyprian's characteristic stress on unity is linked to this point: "Our prayer is public and common; when we pray, we pray not for one, but for the whole people, because we, the whole people, are one."[6]

Even more dramatically expressed, this link between praying and the form of life appears in Origen's treatise, *Peri Euches*:

> The man who links together his prayer with deeds of duty, and fits seemly actions with his prayers is the man who prays without ceasing, for his virtuous deeds or the commandments he has fulfilled are taken up as a part of his prayer. For only in this way can we take the saying "Pray without ceasing" as being possible, if we can say that the whole life of the saint is one mighty integrated prayer.[7]

The contexts of praying differ greatly. Not only is there liturgical and "free" prayer, but also varieties such as penitential, petitionary, contemplative, eucharistic, and so on, each stressing different emotions in different circumstances. But the meaning and point of praying, and the question of how one "means" what one says in praying is best answered in relation to the form of life in which praying occurs. This does not make prayer a "work," though some are always ready to do so. Quite the contrary, prayer gains meaning for the believer in community as it manifests the primal dispositions of the life of faith within a concrete mode of existing. A theology of grace must always show how one's way of being in the world is part of the communal environment which continually receives its own life as a gift. For our purposes we can assert that meaning in prayer is determined by the lived "Christian worldview," not an imagined possibility, but as a concrete way of being disposed toward the world in intention and action.

Underlying prayer of whatever variety within the Christian life is the conviction that "this is the will of God in Jesus Christ for you." While such a conviction brings fear and trembling when one dares continue prayer in the absence of lively faith, it also points to the joyful thought that God is at work in the very perseverance of the people. The Spirit works even in our inability to pray as we ought.[8] The capacity to "mean" what one prays is not cultivated by mere force of will, or even by strength of character. It is finally known only as something given by faith. Recognizing it as a gift is necessarily dependent upon living the Christian life, in season and out of season. To mean what one prays is not gained by mere intellectual grasp of theology; it is part of living out certain emotions which are regulated by the Christian teachings and the Christian story of God and the world.

Most importantly, the capacity to mean what one prays has not to do with the intensity of "feelings" caused in praying, but with the genuineness and the depth of emotion inhering in that way of life. As C. S. Lewis said, "Emotional intensity is in itself no proof of spiritual depth. If we pray in terror, we shall pray earnestly; it only proves that terror is an earnest emotion. Only God himself can let the bucket down to the depths in us."[9]

There is nothing so obvious, yet nothing so problematic for Christian prayer and worship, as the fact that the shaping and expression of human emotion are necessary to such activities. The language of prayer and worship gives expression to the community's human experience and to the range of life before God. This is especially evident in the psalms which are paradigms for liturgical and devotional prayer:

The Lord reigns; let the earth rejoice;
Let the many coastlands be glad!

Make a joyful noise unto the Lord. . .

Why are you cast down, my soul, and why are you disquieted with me?
Hope in God; for I shall again praise him, my help and my God.

You sweep men away; they are like a dream,
Like grass which is renewed in the morning;
In the morning it flourishes and is renewed,
In the evening it fades and withers.

The language in these instances has to do with emotions which target elemental facts of our existence. The range of prayer is the range of elemental patterns in our life - emotions linked with birth and death, sin and terror, gratitude and heartbreak, despair and hope, wretchedness and happiness. Such emotions are not simply named in our prayers and songs and liturgical texts, they are portrayed often dramatically. They are both asserted and expressed in language which is heightened. The language of prayer is embedded in the fundamental gestures of the self and the community. Communal prayer is linked with characterizing actions of the gathered assembly.

How natural and tempting it is to regard the real phenomena of faith as something "inner" and hidden, and the rites and language of prayer and worship as a public instrument or vehicle by means of which faith expresses itself. Thus there arises, as we have noted, a great tendency to divide our thinking about prayer and affections into inner feelings and "outer" world and gestures. Various forms of pietism and movements of renewal of prayer and religious experience often divorced or separated the inner prayer of the heart from the language of the liturgy. For many there is clear dichotomy between "real" prayer and "formal" external language in worship. This has perpetuated a misleading picture of the relationship between prayer and emotions which I should like to consider in this section.

Emotion-terms are part of a proper description of the life of prayer: thanksgiving, adoration, awe, remorse and sorrow, pity and compassion. These are features of the form of life in which praying has meaning and point. To take up a prayerful way of being in the world requires readiness; the language of prayer and worship not only expresses such emotions, it also forms and critiques, it shapes and refines these emotions in persons. Our descriptive problems, however, stem from the fact that so much of our habitual way of regarding "emotion" in prayer and worship is systematically unclear.

Most of us commonsensically think of an emotion as something inside us which we "feel." An emotion word like "anger" or "joy" seems, on the surface, to refer to an inner episode of feeling. In the context of discussing religious experience we always begin to regard emotions as special kinds of complex inner sensations. Furthermore, it is common to build up prejudice against emotions regarded in this light. After all, do we not speak of emotions as "clouding, disturbing, warping" or distorting persons' perceptions and judgments? We speak of people not being in control of their emotions. To be emotionally upset, emotionally involved, emotionally biased, or emotionally exhausted usually refer to a disorganized or poorly functioning individual. Then, too, we speak of being "overcome" by emotion, or being seized by emotions, thereby suggesting that we are merely passive in the grip of strong emotions. The classical religious prescriptions to put away the "passions" reinforces this picture.

But such emotions are not simply complex sensations. This becomes clear when we ask "Where is the joy?", "Where is the remorse, or the gratitude?'' We can locate sensations and bodily feelings this way, but emotions such as joy, remorse, grief, or gratitude belong properly to the whole person. They require thoughts and judgments in order to be what they are and do in human life. While we *use* emotion-terms to refer to ''feelings,'' they are not simply names for inner episodes. More importantly, not every instance of having an emotion or expressing emotion has to do with distorted judgment or loss of discernment and reason.

In speaking of emotion and prayer, then, we must be careful not to think in terms of simple cases of emotion such as anger or fear which often go together with disturbing thought and judgment. We cannot take such cases as standard emotions. The standard cases of emotion are not just anger, fear, rage and hate any more than the standard cases of ''weather'' are rainy and stormy days.

The Christian life has depth and shape precisely because there is a conceptual link between the central emotions in prayer and the way of regarding, assessing, and judging the world and the things therein. Being capable of love, hope, remorse, and gratitude require much more than the ability to ''feel,'' though we do not wish to deny the fact that prayer may bring intense periods of ''feeling'' such emotions. In this latter sense we ''bear'' our emotions in such different ways, since feeling emotion differs according to temperament, physiology and other bodily circumstances. But we should not mistake the task of shaping and expressing emotions in Christian prayer and worship with making persons conform to some personality profile. Not all persons show the emotions of joy and thankfulness, for example, with the same behavioral intensity even though they may be equally capable of Christian joy and thanksgiving.

Certainty about having the same depth emotions in common results from sharing in the same patterns of prayer, in the same liturgical actions such as gathering at the Lord's table, and finally in the same story about the world. ''Expressing'' certain beliefs and ways of regarding the world in the language of prayer requires having the appropriate emotions. The language of prayer provides us with cases in which emotions are given articulation and expression in language which asserts what is believed about God and the believers in relation to God.[10]

When we pray and mean ''Have mercy on me, O God, according to your steadfast love...according to your mercy, blot out my transgressions'' we find descriptions of our sinful life before God as part of the language of confession. Descriptions such as this, which tell us what is believed about God, are logical features of the language of aspiration, desire, and longing.

These are not untypical cases of liturgical language. Time and again, the emotion - love and fear of God, joy, remorse for disobedience, and so on - is specified and made clear only by language which attributes features to God's being. In the standard collect forms of prayer, as we have seen, the petition is dependent upon the characteristic of God singled out in the opening ascription "Almighty God, unto whom all hearts are open, all desires known, and from whom no secrets are hid: Cleanse the thoughts of our hearts..." In the final prayer of the Notre Dame Morning Praise office is another example: "We acknowledge that we are the work of your hands, O God our Father, may we not be silent in the face of your splendor but unite with all creatures, seen and unseen, in hymning your praise, through Jesus Christ . . ."[11] The language of prayer and worship shapes us in the specific emotions by ascribing what is believed about God to God.

One more thing must be said. We have been speaking of the meaning and point of prayer from a human point of view, attempting to throw some light on the nature of the central rule-keeping activity of the language and affections of the Christian faith. When such anthropological descriptions are given, we must also see that adequate and "truthful" worship in the Christian community leads to a theological assertion: worship is also the activity in which God the Holy Spirit works. In light of John's gospel we may claim that worship is the ongoing prayer of Christ in the Church. This reminds us of the central paradox of Christian life and worship: Christ prays for the world in and through our prayers in his name. Those who pray with him are participants in his relationship with the other members of the Trinity - the relationship of love and self-giving which is the Holy Spirit. To pray with him is to be given the gift of life *within* God's own self-giving. Though this way of putting the matter has in the past implied a certain ecclesiology, I think it can be shared by all as signalling the connection between the human and the divine in true Christian prayer.

This point cannot made casually. It is not an ordinary piece of information. It speaks a mystery hidden from the eyes of the world even in a "world come of age." It links a human activity with the mystery of God's hiddenness from the plain view, from the indifferent and passionless attitude toward the world.

Worship, then, can be regarded as a time and place where language about God shapes and expresses human persons, but in such a way as to reveal the meaning and point of speaking about God. It is a way of existing and a way of understanding. As George Herbert, the seventeenth-century Anglican priest and poet, makes clear in "Prayer": it is the Church's banquet, a heart in pilgrimage, a place for sinners, a life's range of emotions and indeed "something understood."[12]

Many contemporaries who find religious practices embarrassing or repressive, or "overly emotional" often reject belief in God on these grounds. It is often said that the judgments of religious believers are distorted and beclouded. But is it a matter of having a distorted picture of oneself and the world when one can rejoice in suffering, or give thanks continuously for life as a gift? Is it a matter of illusory claims about the world to wrestle with meaning and truth in light of God? God can easily become a *deus ex machina* for supporting what is already comfortably believed about life. But this surely is an abuse of belief and prayer because the linkage between believing that we are sinful and that God forgives us, and the capacity to repent and rejoice is anything but self-delusory, at least, if we pray "without ceasing" in the sense outlined in the first section of this chapter.

Clarity respecting connections between emotion and prayer is not the same as emotional clarity by virtue of praying with faith. What clarity has been gained here is not to be confused with self-clarity which comes from praying in community the words of the psalm: "Search me, O God, and know my heart . . ." Or, at the other side of the emotional range of prayer, we have these concluding lines from St. Cyprian's *De Dominica Oratione:* "Here below let us offer ceaseless prayer and gratitude - for in the kingdom we shall pray and give thanks to God for ever."[13]

This primary religious affection and its companions, which together constitute the fabric of Christian life, call for a more detailed exploration.

four

The Christian
Affections

Gratitude And Giving Thanks

Christian prayer is first and last praising and giving thanks to God. Learning to pray is learning what it means to bless the name of God. This is not a natural impulse in the sense that it is on the lips of everybody. Learning to speak the name of God with all that befits praise requires time and understanding. While the instinct to praise someone we love and in whom we delight is part of our natural life, learning to give thanks to God for gifts bestowed requires coming to know what those gifts are. The inclination to thank another person when gifts are given is natural, but in Christian prayer it finds a new object. Thanking God is not simply a natural outcome of perceiving the world with an untrained eye and heart, though awe and wonder and terror may be. From the onset we must assert that Christian teachings about God are involved in learning to pray. Such teachings always shape and refine emotional capabilities which develop in the normal course of life. In short, the Word shapes our subjectivity in the direction of God.

One has not fully understood what the concept of Christian gratitude is until one sees the point of spontaneity in giving thanks in the midst of life. The capacity to discern events and persons in the field of human experience as occasions for gratitude is part of the understanding of who is addressed; for God is the source of every good and perfect gift.

In speaking the Name in gratitude and praise, we acknowledge that God is the one worthy of praise and blessing. In learning to be thankful we learn the attributes of God, beginning with love and mercy, but also in due season, justice and judgment as well. It may be easier, of course, to thank God for love than for divine justice. The latter takes a more mature faith,

40

and a deeper comprehension of the ways of divine love. To say with Job, "though God slay me, yet shall I praise him," pushes our understanding to the point of extremity.

It is irreligious to take the world for granted, and to remain unaffected by its grandeur and misery. To such a passionless and indifferent frame of mind, the world is neither grand nor tragic. Christian prayer, by contrast, teaches us that everything is a gift given in God's freedom. The thanksgiving of the Christian, as Romano Guardini remarked, "consists in accepting life, with ever-growing awareness, as God's gift."[1] The concept of God as creator and redeemer of the world is embedded in the affections of gratitude and praise. Learning how to give thanks with the Scriptures involves mastering the concept of God as creator and redeemer.

Coming to have the capacity for gratitude for those things truly worthy is not merely a pious behavior trait; it is essential to our humanity. Human maturity is bound up with the capability for gratitude. This link between a central feature of Christian prayer and a trait of human moral maturity must not be taken lightly. So far as prayer is first and last speaking God's name in praise and gratitude, it is part of the discovery of our humanity as well. This double journey - into God and into the depths of our humanity - characterizes all of the basic Christian affections we are examining. Again Guardini: "It is therefore of the utmost importance that we should learn to give thanks. We must do away with the indifference which takes all things for granted, for nothing is to be taken for granted - everything is a gift. Not until man has understood this will he truly be free."[2]

This is particularly clear in the Jewish concept of prayer as *berakah,* or "blessing," which underlies all Christian forms of thanksgiving. Consider some examples: "Blessed be thou, O Lord, King of the universe, who bringest forth food from the earth." "Blessed be thou, . . . who exaltest them that are lowly." "Blessed be thou . . . who clothest the naked."[3]

The point of these prayer forms is to provide a sustaining activity of appreciating and acknowledging all God's gifts, each in it own particularity. Every occasion is identified as manifestation of God's love. The continued glorification of the Name in every circumstance forms a kind of contemplative praise of all God's works in creation.

In order to understand the Hebrew conception of God, the believer has to enter into the *pervasive* affection of gratitude and praise. The theological claim inherent in such prayers is that because God has created, we respond first as God's creatures. But in exercising the primordial affection of gratitude, we come more and more to learn of God's ways.

The eucharistic prayers of the Church developed in large measure along the pattern of extended *berakoth*, thus becoming "great thanksgivings." The structure of these prayers also reveals a narrative of God's works. It is not a matter of simply recalling of past events. What is remembered and recited is part of the present reality and an utterance of praise and thanksgiving. "It is right . . .always and everywhere to give thanks to you," as the *Book of Common Prayer* proclaims. This language of address both forms and expresses the life-orientation of all whose hope and faith are fixed upon God.

What is believed about God is enacted and celebrated in the remembering as a present reality. It calls forth the deep emotions in which are concentrated the history of a people. While there are differences on individual occasions between thanksgiving and praise, in Jewish and Christian prayer they are mutually involving. The offering of thanksgiving to God for "thy goodness and lovingkindness" is directed in such a manner as to "show forth thy praise." What begins as thanking God for specific things ends in giving praise for God's goodness and mercy, hence for God's glory. In the classical eucharistic prayers of the first six centuries, praise of God's glory governs the opening prefaces and gives way to offering thanks for God's mighty acts.

All this is present embryonically in the simple child's prayer of thanks as well. As faith matures in its understanding of God and the awareness of cosmic dimensions in these beliefs and affections, the simple gratitude for small things intermingles more and more with praise and glory for God's own being in itself.

C. S. Lewis has a typically trenchant discussion of his struggle to understand why praise of God was so important. He admits that he was at first put off by the thought that God should demand this. It distressed him that in addition to gratitude, reverence, and obedience, he also had to participate in "a perpetual eulogy." It seems to Lewis that God must be above such demands for gratification. But he had overlooked the fact that all deep enjoyment overflows into praise unless it is deliberately prevented. This is simply a fact in human life. Lovers praise the beloved, citizens their heroes, and religious believers their saints. Furthermore he observed that the "most balanced and capacious minds, praised most, while the cranks, misfits, and malcontents praised least."[4] He concluded that the psalmist's enjoying of praise was simply a call for what all healthy persons do when they address that which they truly care about and revere. "We delight to praise what we enjoy," Lewis remarks, "because the praise not merely expresses but completes the enjoyment; it is its appointed consummation."[5]

Our understanding of gratitude and the act of giving thanks to God is incomplete without this intimate connection with praise. There is in all the great prayers of the Church an overflowing of thanksgiving into praise and joy. Praise too, sweeps up specific occasions of gratitude, naming them in its song. There is a mutuality of affective tone here. A proper understanding of the object of true praise attunes our hearts to the grace of God's gifts.

Such glory and grace are not only a feature of what God has wrought in history, they are part of the very being of God. Grace and glory are never exhausted by our gratitude and praise. This is because even in God's self-communication to the world, the divine being remains veiled, inexhaustible, incomprehensible. Yet we know the divine life to be one of glory and grace. These concepts allow non-presumptive claims to be made about God. We cannot know the very substance of God. Claims to know the "substance" fail to acknowledge and honor who God is in being revealed.

There is here an important connection between grace and gratitude which helps define the concept of human sin. One of the most acute insights on this relation is found in Karl Barth: "Grace and gratitude belong together like heaven and earth. Grace evokes gratitude like the voice an echo."[6] They belong together in such a way that the failure of gratitude is itself a transgression, a sin against the creator. It is failing to ascribe honor and glory due God's name. Hence, claims Barth, "Radically and basically all sin is simply ingratitude - man's refusal of the one but necessary thing which is proper to and is required of man with whom God has graciously entered into covenant."[7]

At the close of the last chapter we referred to an extraordinary phrase in Cyprian's treatise on prayer concerning ceaseless praise. Lewis comments on this doctrine that heaven is a state in which angels and the whole host are eternally employed in praise of God. The only way to grasp what the doctrine really means, he says, requires that

> We must suppose ourselves to be in perfect love with God - drunk with, drowned in, dissolved by, that delight which, far from remaining pent up within ourselves as incommunicable, hence hardly tolerable bliss, flows out from us incessantly again in effortless and perfect expression, our joy is no more separable from the praise in which it liberates and utters itself than the brightness a mirror receives is separable from the brightness it sheds.[8]

The fullest praise in our lives is reserved for the most worthy objects. Here one is reminded again of Jonathan Edwards' stress on the moral

excellency and beauty of God as the supreme object of all holy affections.
The more excellent and worthy the object of human reverence and delight,
the more intense the praise and gratitude will be. This *motif* is found in
different guises in Aquinas and in early theologians such as the Cappadocians.

Lewis links praise with beatitude in this remarkable sentence:

> "If it were possible for a created soul fully . . .to 'appreciate,' that is to
> love and delight in, the worthiest object of all, and simultaneously at every
> moment to give this delight perfect expression, then that would be in
> supreme beatitude."[9]

This is the root of all elation and experienced joy in the religious life.
There are moments in which sustained thanksgiving and praise may allow
us an experiential taste of such completion. This is an experience of the
God's Realm. But such experiences in this life are always partial, "through
a glass darkly," never fully beholding the realm of God. Such moments,
which may even be ecstatic, are significant for faith only if they kindle the
deeper passions of the soul.

When we experience such heightened affection, the whole disposition
of faith is focused and strengthened. This is the respect in which the
"enjoyment" of prayer is crucial to the maturation of faith. Our problem
is that such moments often cause us to want to "make three booths" there
on such an experiential Mount of Transfiguration. But the life of thanksgiving and praise is also connected to humble service and to the ordinary world
with all its needs and hidden grace. The movements of luminosity and
vision are not ours to manage or to package. We can expect such periods
of intensity if our prayer, both communal and alone, is faithfully grounded
in the Word and sensitive to the promptings of God the Holy Spirit. It would
be strange, indeed, if someone claimed to be grateful to God and full of
praise, yet never felt grateful nor was swept into the exhilaration of praise.

> *All you who worship the Lord, bless the Lord.*
> *Sing him praise, and give him thanks,*
> *for his love endures for ever.*[10]

Experiencing this is a function of continuing practice of these exercises in
everyday life.

Gratitude is one of the defining affections of the Christian life.
Because it requires a love and reverence for its object, it is a "happy"
emotion. To be grateful for the gifts which are bestowed rules out being
miserable for having received them. The giver of the gift cannot be regarded
with indifference or disgust if the receiver of the gift is truly grateful.

Gratitude in all its healthy forms requires a willing and happy dependence upon another. Someone who is completely independent of all need, or who at least thinks so, does not learn the affection of gratitude. The ingrate has no "sense" of happy dependency upon others. Being grateful involves taking pleasure in the gifts and the giver. Such gratitude flows over into rejoicing in them.

Yet we also know in everyday life that a gift given "with strings" or with the intention of coercing and arousing guilt prevents the thankfulness we have in mind. If the relationship between the recipient and the giver is one of guilty dependence, then gratitude cannot grow. In short, where the gift is not given freely and out of love, unhappy dependencies arise. Our everyday lives are riddled with such difficulties. Most human gift-giving, even by loving parents, arises from a mixture of motives. This is why some persons have difficulty conceiving the kind of gratitude the Christian life requires. Many people, hedged in by circumstances of guilt and anxiety, can make little sense of the idea of a perfect giver who bestows freely and in love. But such social and psychological difficulties are not grounds for rejecting belief in the goodness of God's creating and redeeming love.

It is clear from this that the form of gratitude and thankfulness belonging to Christian prayer cannot be a feeling or mood. Like all genuine gratitude, it requires the ability to think, to refer to things, and to assess critically the objects toward which one's gratitude is to be directed. There are times when we simply "feel glad." These may be part of the affective tone of gratitude, but cannot be part of the stable capacity. We are not actually thankful to anyone when we enjoy such a general sense of well-being as such, even though such experiences may teach us something of the "feel" of gratitude. If thanks is expressed here at all, it is vaguely expressed in phrases such as "thank my lucky stars."

In all natural human thankfulness, there are beliefs and thoughts which target the gift and the giver. Even more, there are reasons for being thankful and for not being thankful. If we think of mature personal friendships, for example, we see that the mutual regard and happy dependency upon loving care is the very reason for the gratitude. If someone should ask, "Why be thankful for genuinely loving friendships?" we find it difficult to reply, not because we lack reasons, but because such a question does not recognize that the mutual regard is a reason.

Even if we understand the pervasiveness and depth of human gratitude as an emotion governing a large range of action and behavior, we still may be puzzled by Christian gratitude. Surely there are situations and events in which we are prevented from giving thanks. Surely evil, pain, loneliness, and death are not "gifts" in any normal sense. Here is where the distinctiveness of the Christian affection emerges.

The "giving thanks in all circumstances" is linked to the particular belief that nothing can separate us from the love of God shown in Christ Jesus. This is, in turn, part of a larger narrative of the continuing intent of God to be faithful to creation and covenant. Such a story encompasses the darkness of life within it - the pain, guilt, terror, and anguish of all those occasions for which we cannot be thankful without denying our humanity. In this sense, Christian gratitude to God is not limited to a simple-minded "count your blessings" view. It is far too momentous. Belief in the God who is on the ground of hope, and whose love extends through suffering beyond death, places a strain on all normal human gratitude and hope. This shows why the Christian affections are not ordinary feelings and emotions elevated to a higher spiritual degree.

Giving thanks to God for the gift of creation, for forgiveness and reconciliation, for eternal life, is something we learn in praying with Scripture. Gratitude is Christologically focused in the New Testament. This involves a kind of formation and shaping of our human passions by the Word. Such formation is part of adopting a way of life in which we learn a different set of wants and needs from our natural ones. Such matters as hungering and thirsting after righteousness arise only in the context of religious redefinitions of life before God.

Here is the heart of the particularity of Christian gratitude and thanksgiving and of all affections which flow forth from and back into our prayers of thanksgiving. In learning new affections and desires, such as longing for the Realm of God, we also come to see why thanksgiving is appropriate in all circumstances of life. This does not require denial of our feelings of anger, terror, or anguish in the face of evil and death. But it does place these experiences within the sphere of life. "The light shines in the darkness and the darkness has not overcome it" (John 1:5). For this we give joyful thanks and praise.

It would be understandable if someone observed that God is the one to whom praise is due, and that the gift bestowed occasions joy, but then go on to say that he or she has no interest or desire for eternal life. That person feels no gratitude, and cannot pray the prayers of thanksgiving. We can understand such indifference; indeed, we are often gripped by it. Coming to have a passionate regard for God as creator and redeemer of the world changes our relationship to the doctrines. To continue in the prayer of thanksgiving and praise in adversity or in good fortune is to understand more and more deeply who God is.

This is the peculiar incorrigibility of religious beliefs and affections which characterize the Christian life. Even when the world is filled with death, we give thanks, for God's love endures forever. Bitterness, despair, and hopelessness are not integral to this form of life. No one should be deceived into thinking this is possible within the scope of human resources alone. Neither should we think of Christian gratitude as living in naive ignorance of the world's tempest and the reality of evil. False and self-deceptive forms of thankfulness abound, and will continue to be propagated in the name of true faith. This does not alter the theological depth of the most primary Christian prayer: to bless the name of God and to grow in gratitude as the mystery of God's life unfolds.

Giving thanks which marks the simple daily prayer finds its culmination and fullest sounding in the eucharistic prayer of the whole people of God. This is a process of growth. It is never a smooth, even progression. It requires beginning again and again. The grammar of this deep affection is shown in its fruits. Praying with the Church is a continual reminder and a training in the beliefs and emotions which focus God's self-giving as the primal gift. It is discipline against forgetfulness.

Gratitude of this sort cannot be gained in a single episode of conversion. It pervades and animates the whole of life because it takes time to unfold in the passing circumstances of temporal existence. Such a growth in gratitude is both a journey into self-knowledge and the knowledge of God. Appreciating who God is issues in sustained doxology, and in perduring joy as well. The interconnection with other Christian affections will emerge in great detail in the sections which follow.

Praying with thanksgiving felt in one's heart is not always possible. But one continues to render praise for divine grace which moves the world toward God. In so doing the ordinary things in life will not be occasions for thanksgiving - injustice, greed, and envy, the strife among peoples, and all the wide hell of our inhumanity and stupidity. For these one weeps and cries out for mercy.

This is why the Christian affection of gratitude gives fundamental direction to all the other affections. To and from thanksgiving and praise flow the whole pattern of intentions and feelings, actions and thoughts, perceptions of self and world. Yet, as we shall see, love is the fountain and chief of the affections in everyday life.

Holy Fear and Repentance

"The fear of the Lord is the beginning of wisdom" This saying from Psalm 111 may seem to many as strangely out of place in a study of the Christian affections. It seems primitive as though it belongs to an earlier and now outdated theology. This idea is reinforced by our contemporary psychological concern to look upon fears as necessarily unhealthy. We have been taught by conventional wisdom to regard human fears as disturbing and distorting forces, often infantile in nature. Modern conceptions of fear as something to be rooted out of our emotional life often leave us with the idea that there ought not to be anything "fearful" in the world. But the world is indeed still a fearful place. Some of our fears are not only rational but justifiable and wise.

There is also a religious notion at work which makes the concept of fear seem out of place in Christian prayer and life. Liberal religious thought regards expressions such as "God-fearing" as automatic signs of a repressed if not fundamentally closed mentality. Since God is love, it is reasoned, how can we properly be admonished to "fear" the Lord unless someone is trying to force us to accept an authoritarian and perhaps capricious picture of God?

Thus the convergence of modern suspicion of human fear and a liberal theology have forced a problem upon us. My reason for defending the affection of fearing the Lord is that it is indispensable to an adequate grasp of who God is.

We begin by noting the larger context of the words from Psalm 111:

He sent redemption to his people;
he has commanded his covenant for ever.
Holy and terrible is his name!
The fear of the Lord is the beginning of wisdom;
a good understanding have all those who practice it.
His praise endures for ever! [11]

It is illuminating to see the connections which are drawn between what God has wrought among people and the holiness and awe with which the name of God is to be regarded. There is a link to the praise due the name of the One who does mighty deeds on earth. These connections form part of the doctrinal background to the fear of the Lord.

In light of what is ascribed to God's revealing and redeeming acts, it is crucial for us to understand that this particular fearing is above all a *practice.* That is, the accent falls not on the experience of fear, but on the exercise of the concept in one's life. What is this practice of the fear of the Lord? Simply put, it is respect and reverence due to the Lord of all things as ruler and sovereign. There is a dimension of God which is beyond our reckoning of good and evil. God cannot be contained and controlled by our conceptions. Neither can the Holy be contained by our emotions. In learning to know God we learn that self-communication does not exhaust the being of the Divine. Learning the honor and fear of the Name is required in our affective understanding of who God is.

There is an appropriate reticence before the holiness of God. We come to understand this in the life of prayer and worship. Holy fear is grounded in the tension we experience and acknowledge between the holiness of God and our own unholiness. The human heart lives with its deceptions, and can resolutely resist the Word and mercy of God. The history of Israel and of the Christian Church amply illustrates the terrible fact of unfaithfulness to the creator. Humanity can fail God's intentions and wound God's heart, but God is not mocked. This is a fearful matter, and one we come slowly to know.

The utter holiness of God brings judgment upon the unholy and the willingly wicked. Thus the fear of those who believe must be distinguished from the fear of those who remain in unbelief and rebellion. Those who pray to God see more deeply the offense of wounded love than those who simply fear the divine wrath of an unknown God. In this sense, the life of prayer rightly brings with it a "fear and trembling." St. Paul echoes this when he admonishes the church to "Work out your salvation with fear and trembling." The practice of this kind of fear is therefore a strand in all one's actions and intention in the life of faith. In it faith and unfaith are often comingled in our struggle to be before God. It is by no means alien to the language of the vocative prayer. Holy fear has its object and occasion in the holiness and the glory of God. This is why it is not a simple feeling or a mood. It is an affective understanding and a regard for the God who remains other than we are, even in coming close to the created.

Holy fear is a disposition toward the God described in Scripture who initiates a covenant, who seeks to restore the broken relationship with the creatures. So this fearing includes a subtle hint of rebellion and resistance, a mysterious dislike of one who is ruler and Lord of all creation. It keeps love and joy from being presumptuous.

The practice of "fear of the Lord" is part of a whole complex pattern in the religious life. Those who take God seriously must make room for ascribing to God the honor due the one described in the great prayers of the

Church: "Holy art Thou, Holy and strong! Holy, immortal One, have mercy upon us." This leads directly to a consideration of penitence and its affective matrix in the Christian life.

The sixth chapter of Isaiah presents one of the most extraordinary examples of the inner connection between ascribing holiness to God and the mingled affections of fear and repentance. Immediately following the acclamation of the heavenly seraphim - "Holy, holy, holy is the Lord of hosts; the whole earth is full of your glory" - the prophet is filled with awesome fear and repentance: "Woe is me! For I am lost; for I am a man of unclean lips, and I dwell in the midst of a people of unclean lips."[12] This aspect of acclaiming God's holiness is preserved in nearly all the eucharistic liturgies in the people's response known as the *Sanctus.*

"Fear in the Lord" is not simply fear of punishment or wrath for those who address God. It is part of a proper understanding of who God is. There must always be a kind of opacity in descriptions of God's being and action. For while we learn that God is merciful and just, we also learn that the divine life is mysterious, veiled, and incomprehensible as well. In being revealed, God remains God. "Truly thou art a God who hidest thyself, O God of Israel, the Savior."[13] This is not a failure of religious vocabulary. Rather, the source of power and glory in God is unfathomable. God can never be an object of idle or curious speculation. As another familiar hymn sings, "Immortal, invisible, God only wise/In light inaccessible, hid from our eyes." This feature of the language of prayer and hymnody expresses with utter lucidity the greatness and majesty of God. This is not because God is indifferent or capricious or unable to be affected by the created; but because the brightness of God's justice, mercy, and love hides the face of the Divine from mortal sight.

The New Testament passage which brings this forcefully to our attention is found in the letter to the Hebrews: "It is a fearful thing to fall into the hands of the living God."[14] Moreover, Jesus's prayer was heard because of his "godly fear." This casts a whole new light on this affection. It is not like inchoate fear or anger which wells up from within us and has no object. It is given shape and place in our lives by virtue of our having learned who God is.

St. Bernard of Clairvaux, in commenting upon the psalm verse cited above, explains that fear and wisdom represent both speculative knowledge and affective knowledge of God:

It is one thing to know many enriching truths, another to possess them. Likewise, knowledge of God is one thing and fear of God, another; what confers wisdom is not knowledge but fear that touches the heart. He who is puffed up because of his learning, by what right can he be called a wise man? One would have to be entirely lacking in wisdom to call those wise who, having acquired knowledge of God, have not honored Him as God, and have not rendered Him thanks.[15]

Holy fear is thus a necessary part of a non-presumptive approach to God. It keeps theology from becoming knowledge *about* God, however brilliant, and focuses our attention upon theology as knowledge *of* God.

In human lives, fear of the Lord cannot be a passing episode. We attribute a great deal of behavior and intention to those whose lives practice this affection. It is a motive for repentance and for the continual ascription of honor. The deeper this kind of fearing grows, the more we know that we cannot grasp God. This point is neglected to the impoverishment of both prayer and theology. Yet even though the living God is fearful, the letter to the Hebrews enjoins: "Therefore let us be grateful for receiving a kingdom that cannot be shaken, and thus let us offer to God acceptable worship, with reverence and awe; for our God is a consuming fire."[16]

Yet none of this can occur in isolation from learning that God loves and forgives. Terror and cowering, crushing guilt are ruled out as appropriate affections in this kind of holy fear. Respect, humility, and grief over one's sins are ruled into the grammar of this affection. The life of prayer requires a great emotional range precisely at this point. Many Christians' experience in prayer is far too domesticated and narrow. Presumptive closeness and false intimacy with God is often the result. Christian affections such as gratitude and love must allow for a holy and godly fear so that the substitution of mere "chumminess" with God for genuine intimacy may be avoided. Mere warm-heartedness in prayer is too domesticated to respect the otherness and sovereignty of God. The "*Abba*" of Jesus' own prayer, as I indicate in chapter seven, contains such godly fear within it.

"Create in me a clean heart, O God" - so the psalmist sings in Psalm 51. We learn this ever anew. The need for forgiveness never ends; not because we are intrinsically base and rotten, nor because we are incapable of responding in love to God, but because we are incapable of responding in love to God, but because our complicity in the human ways of earth is inevitable. The affectional pattern of repentance flows from the acknowledgment of sin before God. To have a contrite heart is to be moved with sorrow and grief over one's waste of God's gifts. Like all of the defining affections of the Christian life, it cannot be a mood or set of guilt feelings. "Repentance as turning to the mercy of God is set precisely in tension with remorse and dwelling within guilty feelings. If we stop simply at feeling remorse, we have not entered into the deeper inner life of repentance and forgiveness. Repentance, as Max Scheler pointed out, is "a purposeful movement of the mind in relation to guilt, aimed at whatever guilt has accumulated in the human being."[17] True repentance reconfigures the past, and forgiveness replaces guilt with gladness.

The function of prayers of confession and acts of contrition, then, is to continue to shape and to express the requisite movement of the heart and mind and will toward wholeness before God. Without it the gifts of God are not fully received and integrated in our lives. The joy which issues in true repentance is over the recovery of the gifts for which the Christian community continually offers thanks and praise. Here we see the organic relationship among the primary Christian affections.

Certain traditions have fostered a range of attitudes and emotions connected with God as stern lawgiver and humanity as totally depraved. A question must be asked of such views: are these beliefs and their attendant pattern of affections adequate to the whole Christian message? Surely not. "Feeling contrite," and having a conviction of sin may be part of repentance in given cases, but these cannot be essential characteristics, since even here self-deception is possible in the midst of intense experiences. The continuing prayer of the Christian life is characterized not by these dark affections, but by an ever-deepening knowledge of God's holiness and gracious turning to us. The language of life and prayer must show this continuing tension between the need of forgiveness and the acceptance of God's freely offered reconciliation.

Thus it is that prayer is acknowledgment of who we are in the sight of God. To address God and to mean what we pray is to recognize the difference between who God is and what we are. Such affectional recognition, whether it comes as an intense shock or as a gentle stream of tears, itself leads to freedom, to the full dignity of our life before God. For the most part, this recognition dawns gradually as we discover over time the frailty and malleability of our own will, and the mixed motives which govern our actual lives. Confessional modes of prayer are essential to the continuing rediscovery of our humanity as gift from God. Over a lifetime we may learn truly to fear and truly to rejoice in the reconciliation given by grace to faith.

Joy and Suffering

The pattern of life portrayed in the New Testament and given expression in the chief prayers of the Church may strike the nonbeliever as peculiar with respect to joy. The lives of the saints, official and unofficial, exhibit this peculiarity in a marked degree. The emotional life of the Christian seems to be in conflict with conventional wisdom - especially with respect to these primary affections. There is an incorrigibility about them. Put another way, there is a strange independence of these affections from normal circumstances of good and bad fortune.

The case of joy and rejoicing in the Christian life is striking - though we could say the same of gratitude, fear, hope, and love, as well. Ordinarily we expect rejoicing in life when things go well and good fortune is at hand. Someone rejoices naturally over an unexpected reward, or over a new piece of music, or simply because a paycheck has increased. Healthy children are a cause for rejoicing; and surely these days, a lasting marriage is too. Illness and tragedy bring grief, depression, or despair - not joy. But the Christian concept of joy shows a difference from these natural affections. Not that the believer cannot rejoice in natural surroundings, too. The singular feature of Christian rejoicing is that it occurs even in the midst of suffering, pain, and tribulation - even in the midst of grief. This may seem to many people to be either a deceit, a mistake, or something which may require therapy to overcome.

St. Paul admonishes his readers to "rejoice always." Even though he speaks of death and his own anguish, his joy continues unabated. This is no accident, nor is it a function of his own temperament or personality. The continuing in joy of which he speaks is part of the logic of faith. There is a conceptual relation between what the Christian believes about God and prays, and this capacity for joy. The language which describes the world as God's creation and the arena of the divine mercy is related *internally* to the ability to rejoice in all circumstances - even in the midst of suffering.

The praise of Christian prayer is permeated with the note of joy: "The Lord reigns! let the earth rejoice." The peculiar character of this joy is not that it is a mood, but that it is a persistent way of assessing one's life in light of what God is doing. As in the case of gratitude, we must ask what the joy is about and what its grounding is. The answer given in the life of prayer and human relationship is joy *in God.* It is therefore a savoring or taking delight in God in and through the concrete circumstances of existence.

Christian joy is one of the happy emotions because it is part of praise and delight. Its stability is related to a particular set of reasons for rejoicing. The Christian description of the world is that of a world created and redeemed, yet still in travail for its completion. The concept of God which is exercised in prayer and life requires that this view of life be grasped in the affections and held fast. This kind of joy is not the ordinary circumstantial kind. It does not fluctuate with pleasure and pain, or with the changing tide of events. Just for this reason, it must learn patience in light of the feelings of anger, hurt or grief which we experience in the fluctuations of life. The joy is not an easy one, nor does it exact a cheap covering over of pain, suffering, and death. It does focus our lives before God, however. This way of viewing ourselves and the world disciplines and regulates various natural passions and feelings.

The particularity of Christian joy, then, is in the object of rejoicing. The structures and rhythms of Christian prayer are such that the very recalling, remembering, and retelling of the story of God occasions the joy, though such prayer be in the midst of strife. Such a joy requires persistence in the images and teachings of the faith, but also a capability of abiding personal disappointments and triumphs which come and go. There is a way of learning from adversity and tribulation implied in this joy. In this way, suffering the world itself becomes integral to the deeper joy of which the psalmist and, indeed, all of Scripture speaks. To know God in all things is to have God as one's joy and delight, even though all earthly delights pass away with the morning's freshness.

Rejoicing in God is no mere passing episode since it requires letting ourselves learn by trials. It is precisely a way of living at full stretch in the world of pain and gladness. Its very form of life is the rejoicing. Christian prayer is placed over against our natural desires and delights in this sense. It depends upon our continual remembrance that the Christian faith is born in the tension of suffering and joy, of cross and resurrection. The language of joy and of rejoicing we receive in Scripture must always be read against the backdrop of the life of suffering.

The reason for all this is found in the God whose purpose is revealed in the dying and rising of Jesus of Nazareth. This God is known to us in learning the paradox of glory laid aside. We are moved to praise by this glory, for the life of God which remains inexhaustible. But this mystery of the inner life of God is not separated from rejoicing in what has been done in the incarnation, life, suffering, death, and resurrection of Jesus Christ. Adequate Christian prayer thus conjoins the joy over what God has accomplished for us with the joy in the excellence and beauty of the very life of God.

Karl Barth has made this connection between Christian joy and the glory of God both vivid and forceful. The special element in God which permeates all our gratitude, awe and wonder - and our obedience in service as well - with joy is the fact that the fellowship God offers is *intrinsically joyful.*

> The special element to be noted and considered is that the glory of God is not only great and sublime or holy and gracious . . .it is a glory that awakens joy, and is itself joyful. It is not merely a glory which is solemn and good and true . . .Joy in and before God . . .has an objective basis. It is something in God.[18]

It is the form of God's glory which is the special joy. In recognizing this we see why Christian joy has a permanency. It is not founded on the changing delights and disappointments of the temporal life.

All this being said, I can now assert that learning Christian gratitude is also to learn Christian joy. The heart is formed in both these affections to the extent that God's glory is recognized and worshipped - both the glory of God's inner being and the paradoxical glory of the cross and resurrection. To glorify the Name in prayer and worship and life is to rejoice in both the fact of God's being and in God's gracious turning to the world.

The Christian affection of joy is not one more emotion among others; it is the very manner in which we are grateful and the manner in which we offer ourselves to God and neighbor. Yet this joy is never complete because the object of our worship is never fully given to us within the limits of temporal life. Prayer is also eschatological. It anticipates the fullness of joy in the coming Reign of God which liberates us from our inordinate loves and desires in the world. Such anticipation also frees us from unhappiness and despair in the disappointments, pains and sufferings of our existence. In this sense, the joy in God is both inconceivable to us, and the most attractive aspect of the life of prayer. Our hearts are drawn, even by the very thought of it, away from the bondage to affliction and misery. Such a rejoicing is part of mature thankfulness in response to God's love.

This kind of joy is a condition for making sense of human existence. It is set at odds with our normal run of enjoyments and joys. Jesus remarks that in the world his followers will have tribulation, but nevertheless are to be of good cheer, for ''I have overcome the world.'' This is not done through mere courage. Courage may be called for in the exercise of faith, but the joy is not a function of the will. Rather we are to welcome the world with its pain and suffering because it is into that world that God's glory comes in the form of a servant. To ignore the suffering of the world in the name of gratitude and joy violates and trivializes the message of Christianity. The corporate memories of God's dealing with humanity include the darkness and the evil of the world. The joy of the resurrection is a sham without the agony of Gethsemane and the reality of the cross. To be afflicted in the world where powers of life and death contend is precisely our identification with the redemptive and suffering love of God in Christ. This passion of God is revealed to eyes of faith. The hidden glory of God is in that death and sin are overcome not by force, but by suffering love. This is a strange and terrible beauty which draws us to a joy the world cannot know or give.

Love of God and Neighbor

"But the greatest of these is love." This familiar phrase from St. Paul's hymn to love in I Corinthians summarizes what I wish to say about the affection of Christian love. The double command Christ gives to love God and neighbor focuses the Christian life of emotion, virtue, and understanding. For this reason all the other affections find their orientation here. Wisdom as a true "knowing God" presupposes the ardor of love for God. St. Thomas Aquinas, echoing the Augustinian tradition, speaks of the relation between enkindled love for God and the illumination of the intellect. "Ardor precedes illumination, for a knowledge of truth is bestowed by the ardor of charity."[19]

In Edwards' *Treatise* we find repeated emphasis upon the centrality of the gracious affection of love. It is evident in Scripture, he contends, that "the essence of all true religion lies in holy love . . .For love is not only one of the affections, but it is the first and chief of the affections, and the fountain of all the affections."[20] This may be read as a gloss on I Corinthians 13. For the life of Christian prayer, the apex of faith and hope is love of God and neighbor.

We will misunderstand the scope and nature of love if it is taken in isolation from the whole pattern of primary affections I have been exploring. It is never a disembodied love born solely in contemplation. It is vulnerable and costly. To love God is to risk *being known.* The love of neighbor which flows from this is costly in another way. As C.S. Lewis observes, the love of neighbor we learn in intercessory prayer must be a real and costly love, with deep feeling for the sins in spite of which we love the sinner - no mere tolerance or indulgence...Next to the Blessed Sacrament itself, your neighbor is the holiest object presented to your senses. If he is your Christian neighbor, he is holy in almost the same way, for in him also Christ, the glorifier and the glorified, Glory Himself, is truely hidden.[21]

Within the scope of Christian prayer, then, we detect a particular kind of ordering principle. Prayer begins with praise and thanksgiving and issues in love. This is love of God in whom we rejoice and before whom we confess in holy fear, and love of neighbor who is the mysterious bearer of God's glory hidden in humility. Particular prayers for others show forth the grammar of this dual love. The neighbor is seen as an object of God's own love and therefore as one worthy of our care and attention. To intercede is to join with the continuing prayer of Jesus Christ whose life's name was love - suffering and victorious. This theme returns in the last two chapters of this book.

In prayer we meet God coming to us. Loving God is a way of knowing how all things coinhere in God. Thus praying is inseparable from love of God - it is the language of love which completes the relationship God initiates. It is that affection which most closely resembles the inner life of God's own self-giving. No wonder the image of the Trinitarian life of God is found in a society of loving persons.

The love of God for us creates the possibility of prayer. Constancy in the dialogue and communion with God reflects the nature of God, hence we exercise one dimension of this love in adoration and praise, pouring out our lives in service of the neighbor to exercise the other dimension. These are not different kinds of love, just as the great commandment Jesus gives is not two commandments but one: "You shall love the Lord your God with all your soul and mind and strength and your neighbor as yourself." Entering into one requires entering the other. Compassion for the neighbor and adoration of God are not separate intentions of two worlds, they are the modes of intending and receiving the love of God in its double manifestation.

To "lift up our hearts," as the ancient opening dialogue of the eucharistic prayer bids us, is to place ourselves at the disposal of the divine self-giving. In rendering glory to God we learn to glorify the Holy One in all the commonplaces of life. To be formed in the holy affection of love is to respond to the prior love God has for all creatures. It is a condition for recognizing and receiving what God bestows. The more deeply we perceive and exercise this love toward the broken and the hungry, the naked and the imprisoned, the more clearly we are governed by the divine will and drawn toward the Realm of God.

Prayer forms in us the disposition of compassion toward others. This can never be mere sentiment. It is a way of identification with others akin to the care we give to our own existence. Such love is put to the test, whereas "loving feelings" are not. Loving our neighbors requires truthfulness about suffering and evil which befall them and us all. Hence the brokenness of the world is the arena in which we are called by love to practice costly compassion. This is the pattern laid down in the life of the one who teaches us to pray.

In a perceptive article on Kierkegaard's conception of becoming an individual before God, Robert Roberts points out that the Christian affections are by no means the same as the virtues of ordinary ethics. He proposes that

> our "joy in the Lord," our gratitude to God, our love of neighbor, and so on, all have reference to the atoning work of God in the cross of Jesus Christ. The Christian emotions all gain their specific contours from our seeing ourselves as brothers and sisters of Jesus Christ; and such self-perception depends on our hearing and believing his story.[22]

My task has been to offer a grammar of some primary Christian affections which are given shape and expression in prayer. These affections are interrelated, just as the attributes of God are related one to the other. God is understood as a living unity. So too, the life of affections and virtues is unified in the human person by the ground and object of all gracious affections. Each affection is a facet of the life of prayer and is correlated to various attributes of God. Praying to God in, with, and through Jesus Christ directs our lives toward these attributes on different occasions. Entering into such relatedness propels the one who prays into a knowing of God which never ends. Thus, as our lives change so does our love deepen to reveal yet further dimensions of God's mercy, holiness, justice, glory, and love. Unless our praying and our way of being in the world enter upon this emotional range, we cannot begin to comprehend the reality of God.

In the final analysis, neither God nor the one who prays can be analyzed into a discrete series of attributes. But unlike the being of God, our experiences are always partial and therefore subject to tension and one-sidedness. Fear and love of God may coexist, not because of the strength of our affectional understanding, but because of the nature of God toward whom these emotions are directed. Prayer turns us back again and again to praise and thanksgiving, to awe and confession, to rejoicing and intercession, and unifies these in love of God. These are the distinctive marks of Christian life. In them we find an unfolding pattern of primary Christian affections which are the wellspring of feeling, understanding, and acting in the life of faith.

five

Praying And Thinking:
The Work of Theology

An admonition from Bishop Ignatii Brianchaninov should be fastened over the doorpost of our entrance into these pages:

> Do not theologize, do not be carried away by following up brilliant, original, and powerful ideas which suddenly occur to you. Sacred silence, which is induced in the mind at the time of prayer by a sense of God's greatness, speaks of God more profoundly and more eloquently than any human words. "If you pray truly," said the fathers, "you are a theologian."[1]

We begin with a curious question: Can we pray and think about God, too? It awakens a certain puzzlement. We have already said that religious emotions, and the Christian affections in particular, are not simply inexpressible inner episodes. There is a grammar or inner logic about them which can be explored. We both experience our emotions and affections, and talk about them. Our discourse about them cannot substitute for having them (if we try to substitute talk for experience, we are in a sorry state). Yet we may, by reflection, understand the range and power of such affections more clearly than if we only experienced them. Religious affections do not remain in silence. They seek expression in words which portray their object.

But now we inquire about relations between prayer, as the language of the heart, and theology itself. What has praying to God to do with thinking *about* God? Some readers may already complain "With all the emphasis upon the Word and words, you have intellectualized prayer; just the way theologians always intellectualize God!" This complaint arises most frequently from the conviction that theology is, by definition, an academic substitution of words about God for the Word of God. By analogy, attempts to understand prayer may seem to substitute language about prayer for the language of prayer. There is fair warning here.

The first thing to notice is that Scripture itself intermingles language about God and language addressed to God. The Psalms, for instance, always have in their background descriptions of what God has done in history. The prayers of the New Testament Church function in the context of a complex web of language which reflects upon the One to whom the prayers are addressed, whether in John's gospel, Paul's letters or the Book of Revelation. So we should not be too hasty in drawing a hard and fast line between "language of" and "language about." The point at issue is what each idiom of language is used *for*.

In the second place, it is quite possible to think prayerfully and to pray thoughtfully. Some kinds of theological reflection are infused with the very spirit of prayer. We find this especially in the early Fathers of the Church, in mystical writers, and even in some contemporary theologians.[3] Perhaps the most obvious example is found in the *Confessions* of St. Augustine. The whole tissue of thought is address to God as prayer. To think prayerfully brings theology close to life. Concerning thoughtful prayer, we think immediately of St. Paul's demand for intelligibility in prayer:

> I would rather speak five words with my mind, in order to instruct others, than ten thousand words in a tongue . . . If I pray in a tongue, my spirit prays but my mind is unfruitful...I will pray with the spirit and I will pray with the mind also (I Corinthians 14:14-15)

There are several contrasts relevant to our question, not one simple and obvious dichotomy between praying and thinking. We may pray with understanding or without. We may think about God without being rooted in prayer, or we may think by virtue of continuing to address God.

The point is not to draw a sharp line between the activities of praying and theological thinking. We may pray with understanding or without. We may think about God without being rooted in prayer, or we may think by virtue of continuing to address God.

The point is not to draw a sharp line between the activities of praying and theological thinking, but to examine concrete examples and try to determine whether one is "intellectalizing" God, prayer, or theological teachings.

Consider the connection between three different emotions and thinking. Can we be depressed and think about our depression? Of course; when we think in a depressed mood, our thoughts are depressed. "I wish I weren't feeling this way." "Why am I this way again?" "Nothing matters if I find out." Notice that these thoughts are deeply colored by the state of depression.

In the case of grief, other features of the relation to thinking appear. We focus on thinking about the object of our grief; the loved one lost. The affection directs the form our grieving thoughts take. We may have angry thoughts, or tender thoughts mixed with them. The more overwhelming the grief, the more difficult it is to have clear thoughts at all. Grief is no momentary episode, nor a passing mood. Rather, it governs a wide range of our life and, hence, of our thinking. In the case of mature love, there is another range of things which come with thinking about the beloved. Immediately a range of maturity is involved. Infatuation and puppy love, or strong romantic attractions are each quite different from the love of marriage or deep friendship. The language of love is not an ornament or an external vehicle for thoughts; rather it conveys loving thoughts and is itself part of the behavior of love. The loving brings a particular reflective knowledge with it. But the more mature the love, the clearer and deeper are the thoughts about the relationship with the beloved.

There is an analogy with our primary question in such examples. The relation between praying to God and thinking about God can be illuminated by focusing upon the religious affections. The central and decisive Christian affections require concepts, judgments, and thoughts which yield insight into the nature of God. Since praying both shapes and expresses these deep emotions, the various modes of prayer will reveal something of the nature of the God who is addressed. Thus praising, confessing, giving thanks, adoring, and interceding are modes of being in the presence of God, each with its own cluster of affections.

The sense of God who turns toward us in grace is part of the language and gesture of praise and thanksgiving. Thus, as we saw in chapter four, the eucharistic prayer is itself an extended theology. It is "recital theology." Remembering and thanking God are not parallel processes. Rather, the narrative of the prayer articulates and vivifies appropriate thoughts and affections in the very act of praising and giving thanks. The shape and vitality of the language often shows this dramatically, as in the case of the earliest known eucharistic prayer from the *Didache:*

> Remember, Lord, your Church to save it from all evil and to perfect it in your love . . .(gather) it together from the four winds into your Kingdom which you have prepared for it; for yours are the power and the glory forevermore. Amen.[4]

In addressing another person our thoughts and emotions comprise a single matrix with the utterance. Under normal circumstances we do not say *that* we are praising, or pleading, and *then* say what we think and believe about the person. What we think or believe is part of our praise or pleading. If a misunderstanding arises, then we may separate the thoughts about the person from the affective utterance in which they are expressed. This is also true of prayer. When misunderstandings about God arise, theology emerges as a distinct kind of thought. Theology provides a grammar for the affective content and shape of the praying. Yet theology itself requires that right praise be rendered to God if right doctrine (knowledge of God) is to be preserved.

Theology is a way of understanding the One addressed in prayer. It involves reasoning and reflecting upon the concreteness of prayer in response to the "Thou" of God. Yet theology belongs to a mode of understanding deeper than knowing by reason alone. Since prayer is communion and dialogue involving a relatedness in passion between those who pray and God, theological thinking must exhibit the nature of that relationship in the way it approaches its subject. Hence there is an essentially religious character - as distinct from a purely discursive or detached knowledge - which theology must retain even in its task as reflective knowledge about God. This does not mean that theology is nothing more than quotations from prayer or scripture. Nor does this deny the critical and analytical use of the mind. Put simply, theology must respect its object. "It is not disputation." St. Bernard of Clairvaux once said, "it is sanctity which comprehends if the incomprehensible can, after a certain fashion, be understood at all."[5]

Since theology employs human thinking, it is open to any and all inquirers; but in driving toward understanding its true object, it involves a mode of reasoning which is shaped by the very mystery it seeks to fathom. Though the mystery of God remains incomprehensible to unaided human reason, it nonetheless can be grasped in the mode of religious affections. Love and holy fear of God involve the mastery of certain teachings, concepts, and doctrines which are sustained most vividly by metaphors, images, and stories. These ways of speaking about God are part of the language of liturgy and prayer. The mystery of God's hidden life is evoked and sustained in the affections proper to coming before God.

The problem, then, is not that the life of prayer and worship are incompatible with thinking about God. Rather, the problem is with a false intellectualism in theology. This is the spirit of using the mind for the sake of disputation and conceptual refinement for its own sake. It is inimical to the mode of understanding God as the One to be worshipped. The mind is not to be sacrificed in prayer, though various enthusiasts and fundamentalists make this appear to be necessary. Rather, we are to think in accord with the mystery of God's gracious turning toward us. Even the notion of the mystery of God need not be treated as something irrational. Theology approaches its task by respecting and participating in the language of the vocative. This, I think, is the force behind Karl Barth's assertion: "Theological work must really and truly take place in the form of a liturgical act, as invocation of God, and as prayer."[6]

In discussing love of God and love of neighbor in the last chapter, we drew attention to the connection between loving and knowing. While each of the primary Christian affections is a "way of knowing," the chief of the affections draws our life to full attentiveness before God. Gregory the Great taught that "love itself is knowledge of him in whom it is directed, because in proportion as we love, to that extent we know."[7] This is echoed throughout St. Augustine and other early theologians. The link between believing in God, knowing God, and the affections appropriate to the life of God, is the touchstone for all theological reflection. This means, of course, that such reflection must attentively listen for the living Word of God in Scripture and in worship. Close-to-life theology which springs from the heart and speaks to it, begins and ends in words and affections formed by the Word.

Let us explore the implications of this claim that prayer, communal and individual, is the heart of faith. Such implications are theological as well as pastoral and psychological.

The Orthodox Church is quick to remind us that the theologian is not so much one who knows the history and techniques of theology as one who knows how to pray. Contemporary theology must recover this point. All too frequently the relation between prayer and theology is regarded as a psychological matter. Books on the psychology of prayer abound. But the relation between theology and prayer is also a conceptual matter, for reasons which the following pages will make clear.

For many persons in the Church, and especially for theologians, prayer appears to be a kind of verbal communication of beliefs. For many it is a difficult gesture to make, particularly if praying is regarded as an optional exercise in religious language, a disposable practice inherited from the past. Others, in recovering the experience of prayer, speak of its excitement and freedom from old theological restraints. For some who hold this latter view, the "adventure of prayer" is prized for its spontaneous inspirations that need no doctrinal check and stability. Such persons would do well to heed the warning of Bouyer:

> The Christian who takes without distinction, as divinely inspired, every spontaneous impression, every more or less developed interior reaction of his own spirit face to face with the divine Word, is in greater danger than anyone else of stifling the Spirit by confusing Him with [his] own unconscious caricature.[8]

But both the "optional exercise" and the enthusiast's view fail to grasp the critical function of theology which begins and ends in prayer. If we are to understand more fully the meaning and point of prayer, we must attend to the logic of religious language about God as exemplified in the activity of praying. This, in turn, may illuminate some essential but neglected features of theological inquiry.

The Church prayed before it undertook the formulation of theology, at least in the ordinary sense of that term. Theology, words about God, was formed and shown in and through the worshipping activities of the gathered community, and through writings of instruction for the Christian life. In every sense of the word, the eucharistic prayer was and is the most powerful form of theological assertion known to the Church. It is as essential as the baptismal questions out of which grew the Apostles' Creed. For in these prayers and responses, the Church's corporate memories are recited, and her reason for being is affirmed and enacted.

This reminder is not intended to detract from other more complex and culturally intertwined forms of theology, some of them embryonically present from the beginning. Rather, it stands as a normative reminder to all subsequent efforts at theological formulation that there is, in the life of prayer and work, a primordial context for theological assertions. This is not simply a sociological context; it is a logically required context for meaning and sense-making in theology. Developing a capacity for theological insight and certainty requires an understanding of the conceptual connections between addressing God and speaking about God in the world.

Despite these qualifications, it would be a mistake for us to underestimate the force of this reminder. For those concerned with discerning and living the truth of Christianity, theology must begin and end in prayer. This sounds monastic; and it is, insofar as the preservation of the connection has been historically a self-professed task of monasticism. Yet it has never been completely obliterated in other "schools" of theology, though many times it has been obscured in the name of piety as well as in the name of "objective" theology, or in the name of apologetic relevance. Whenever theology is undertaken with awareness of what praying asks of those who pray, and of the entailments of the life of prayer, it can no longer be a conceptual game. Praying encourages awareness of the inner link between understanding the true God and coming to address God with all one's heart and mind and soul.

It would be both foolish and false to claim that prayer is a substitute for thinking about God. I am not interested in substituting piety of one sort or another for the demands of studying and reasoning. Our current culture is filled with blind pieties already. The Christian *ecclesia* should exercise every effort to avoid contributing more. No, a central task for theological inquiry is to insure that *persons* — not just "heads," nor just "hearts" — keep the internal relations between theology and prayer clear and resilient. When we lose the capacity to use the word "God" in the vocative, we forfeit our ability to speak convincingly to the world in the indicative of theology.

Prayer, whether private or corporate, is not the kind of activity which concentrates attention upon analytic refinement. It concentrates upon God, and concentrates our life before the face of God, and in this it is not merely "emotive," "expressive," or "subjective." It can be a deeply intuitive activity — and much else — precisely because it sustains an insightful context for the stories, the central parables and images, and the concepts and doctrines which are the stuff of theology. Worship, the continuing corporate prayer of the people of God, is itself a rule-keeping activity for the language of belief. It keeps the paradigmatic descriptions of God, the self, and the world in place. In this sense, prayer provides a placement and a ground for disciplined thinking about Scripture and theology. This implies more than the spiritual admonition that prayer is an aid to understanding; it has something to do with the very logic of religious believing.

Let us examine more explicitly some of the main points contained in the foregoing remarks.

Prayer is a logically required context for the utterance of theological truths. This point is not to be confused with the idea that no one can speak theological truth outside the rooms of liturgical activity. Neither does it mean that theology is only what the simple believer already knows. This is a remark about the connections between the concept of truth and the activities in which speech about God is given *religious* force and sense. Christian beliefs about God and humankind function in a specific way of seeing the world. Such a way of seeing is acquired and sustained through learning to worship and to pray. It is precisely in the "shaping" activities of prayer and worship that the language which asserts things about God and humans has its natural home. If we are to understand what is claimed about God, humans, and the world, we must understand what it is to speak this way. If it is to bear truth, speaking about God must have point in human life.

This leads us to a second consideration. *Prayer is the most filling context for asserting things religiously about God.* For persons having religious concerns, worship and prayer provide continual remembrance and training in the language which characterizes God and the world. Having a religious concern is not quite the same as being concerned about theology as a subject matter. Becoming more knowledgeable about the history of Israel, about the history of doctrine, the theology of Rahner or Barth, or about the shifts and shocks of human consciousness is not noticeably increased by spiritual discipline. Such knowledge results from diligence, sensitivity, and hard work perhaps, but rarely by prayer. (I speak here of knowledgeability, not of spiritual discernment.) However, descriptions of God and how the Divine is disposed toward humankind are not objects of inquiry in the same way. Descriptions of and assertions about God occur in religious surroundings, in the environment of common memories, hopes, and covenant. While they may also occur in philosophical treatises, they are not being given a religious use in such contexts. It is in prayer and worship, where we are made capable of using descriptions of God and humans as the very language of our own way of being in the world, that we grasp a key aspect of their logic.

Theological understanding of the Christian faith depends partly on a person's being habituated in the "liturgical" use of religious language. This is a corollary of the second point. Why is this so? Can't intelligent people come to understand Christian theology just as well by reading about the "logic" of prayer or by understanding what theologians have said to systems of theology? No one need deny that many persons claim to understand the truths of Christian theology apart from the use of Christian concepts in their own lives. But here we need to contrast a discursive understanding with a religious understanding. The reason why true theological understanding depends partly upon our training in liturgical uses of religious language is because these uses inform worshippers with the very concepts and capacities in question.

Prayer, rightly practiced, informs the "inquirer after understanding" with the emotional and conceptual abilities connected with religious beliefs. The so-called "objective" study of theology and learning to describe the concepts does not inform in the same way. The struggle to pray and to worship God informs our very persons, and gives a determinate shape to Christian character. This does not mean that everyone who prays can thereby offer an explicit theological understanding. Prayer as dialogue with God need not be expressed in a verbal theology at all. Indeed, many people pray and worship without an interest in *saying* what their "theological understanding" is. Of course prayer and worship of God can also be theologically inadequate or confused, and hence, inarticulate. The crucial point is this: *If* one seeks theological understanding, then part of the achievement is *logically* dependent upon an understanding of self and world born and nurtured in using the language religiously.

The vocative use of the language about God "shows" something about the logic of religious beliefs. Believing that God created the world as sheer gift is ingredient in seeing, assessing, and acting in the world *via* those beliefs and their appropriate emotions and motives. To believe God creates in love is to be responsive to the world in gratitude. The vocative mode of speech in prayer and worship is necessarily self-involving, if one means what one is saying. For example, when we use the language of sin and repentance or the language of gratitude and thanksgiving in addressing God, we exercise those capacities to which we have been referring. Such vocative mode of speech is simultaneously assertive and expressive. "Have mercy on me, O God, according to your steadfast love . . .According to your abundant mercy, blot out my transgressions." One sees this most clearly in the traditional collect forms of prayer. The traditional Collect for Purity begins, "Almighty God, unto whom all hearts are open, and from whom no secrets are hid, cleanse the thoughts of our hearts . . ." Believing that God sees the human heart can never be a neutral belief — its logic involves us personally.

The vocative mode shows the relation between the life of one who prays and the words about God. To use the language of prayer faithfully is to show certain regulating concepts and emotions toward oneself and the world. We can say that it expresses fundamental attitudes, dispositions, and patterns of feeling *given with* that very way of speaking about God. These are not "effects" of believing, but are part of the believing. Such logical features of the vocative connect saying and understanding. For example, "O Lord, you alone know . . ." is an expression which, *in use*, brings the truth about oneself forward — the hidden recesses are open because the concept of being known by the One who searches hearts is being put to work in one's life.

Prayer also has to do with "religious experience." Rightly so. In and through sustained prayer and worship, one comes to have the emotions and dispositions which manifest the belief in God. To love, to fear, and to rejoice in God are signs of believing in God. But the character and activity of the person are central, not simply the experiencing of exquisite episodes of feeling. In the corporate praying of the psalms, we extend our empathies (hence our understanding) to pride, vanity, and vengeance as well as to praise. This gives us more than tolerance or even acute self-understanding, as desirable as these are. If we mean what we say in praying the psalms, it is more akin to an experiential exploration of the doctrine of *simul justus et peccator* than to the evincing of certain feelings. We can be taught by the psalms something of the logic of being both a descendant of the old Adam and a child of the second Adam, condemned by the demand for obedience to precepts, yet released from the impossibility of perfection.

Theology strives to understand the God we encounter and address. Thus in thinking about God, we wish to assert the truth about God, the world, and human existence. This is a legitimate part of theology — forming words about God to tell the truth about things. Constant re-description and clarification of the words (hence, the concepts) is also part of the task. This is why theological thinking must continually return to the communal rule-keeping of its primary images, concepts and narratives. Praying in all its variety is the primal mode of construing and understanding religious beliefs about God.

Prayer and worship are a knowledge of God which should help us say something about our life, under the impress of faith, which will *stand firm.* Praying for understanding of this sort, even with deep sincerity, is not automatically rewarded with theological depth. There is a space between religious insight *per se* and theological refinement. Since theological inquiry can be made to serve several functions — not only a religiously edifying function — we do well to respect the space between the discipline of theology and the practice of the religious life. My effort here has been to clarify some ways in which prayer is a sense-making context as well as an occasion for religious affections.

Theology begins and ends in prayer. This, as it stands, is only a slogan, hinting at an ethos in which theological learning may take place. It is not a sacrifice of the intellect on the altar of personal piety. Rather, it reminds us that whatever conceptual network may be elaborated by various theologies, the indigenous concepts are those which are discerned most clearly in the liturgical life of the faithful. Prayer is *more* than thinking, *more* than "subjective" communion. It is a ground and *telos* for theological reflection. More than this, it is the activity which keeps driving the Christian to live for others in the world. The language of theology describes this world in which it is asserted that God dwells with us — the very world in which we are asked to do justice and mercy, and to love and serve God and neighbor. Praying for the needs of the world is conceptually linked to the disposition to serve the neighbor. To paraphrase Jesus: "Those who say they love God and yet hate their brothers or sisters are liars."

This has been the most rudimentary reflection on why attending to conceptual relations between learning to pray and coming to understand theological concepts may be important for theology. Questions about the relationship between liturgical and private prayer have not been raised here. But I am convinced that part of the current confusion about what constitutes adequate theological method can be traced to an inadequate perception of these basic connections between theological thinking and the life of prayer. "As food is to the body, so prayer is to the soul." And, we might add, to the soul of theology in the life of the Church.

Can we pray and think about God, too? The question is rhetorical, but our comments on the work of theology have been much more. Reflecting upon and with the question, we inevitably return to the embeddedness of language about God in the practices of prayer and worship. The answer to our question is shown in how we speak about God. To a significant degree the strength of any theology is measured by its power to enkindle both understanding and love for its object.

Theology taken in this sense is a critical reflection upon the life and language of faith in God. It is knowledge of God in a special sense. The work of theology which takes its roots seriously is not simply a systematizing of what the Church says it believes. This may be involved. The crucial matter, however, is such discernment of the mystery of God that the depth of our language about God is clear, even to the point of correcting what the Church may believe in a given age. Theology is a series of reminders of what it is to address God properly and with the appropriate affections.

As thinking about God, theology does not supply us with inferences about onotogical news from nowhere. It provides a coherent and consistent view of the God who turns to us and to the created order graciously and freely, with justice and the terrible speed of mercy. But it provides also a grammar for speaking and being in the world befitting who we are in God's love. For the faithful it should state the certainties to which all are entitled; for those who cannot claim belief, theology makes clear what it means to do so.

Theology begins when we first pray. This is the gesture of recognition, however dim or inchoate, of who God is. Theology thus matures as our life with God matures. We say with Evagrius, ''If you are a theologian you will pray truly, and if you pray truly, you are a theologian.''[9] So it is that, despite the complexities and diversions of modernity which cannot be ignored, theology may still be in praise of God. This may lead us back to the path of silence before the greatness and glory of the One who searches our hearts.

Nevertheless, those who struggle to pray and whose faith is in search of understanding, remain in the world. We are situated in time and history. We pray and live within the world's field of forces. To recognize the inner connections between praying to God and thinking about God is only a starting point. In the next two chapters, I explore instances of how the negative theological thinking reviewed here is put to work. In chapter six, I focus upon how we may understand ourselves as creatures responding to the world; in the concluding chapter, upon being formed in Christ by praying with him. These show a movement in the essentially religious character of knowledge of God — an affectional knowing which unites and joins us with God.

six

Praying and Being:
Responding in the World

The reality of prayer, Archbishop Anthony Bloom reminds us, is rooted in the features of human existence:

> Prayer is not simply an effort which we can make the moment we intend to pray; prayer must be rooted in our life and if our life contradicts our prayers, or if our prayers have nothing to do with our life, they will never be alive nor real.[1]

Praying is a worldly activity. By that I do not mean that it is sinful, though it can surely be so (one thinks of Herbert's strong line: "Engine against th'Almightie, sinners towre"). Nor do I mean that it is always "active," for it requires receptivity as well. By worldly I mean that praying is something flesh and blood human beings do in the world. As long as life lasts even the most contemplative persons must pray *here*. John Berryman quips in a poem, "I know You are there, Lord, the sweat is, I am here."[2] Prayer is worldly because, along with its consolations, it is a way of *intending* the world.

The view we have seen unfolding leads to the inner connection between praying and being. How such a form of life confronts the suffering and gladness of the world is, of course, a key question. Spiritual self-deception is always possible because praying is done in the human sphere of forces. Prayer and praise in heaven, we may assume, no longer fall victim to deceit. In hell, self-deception has become a way of life. Prayer that seeks withdrawal from the realm of human forces — social, economic and otherwise — fails to exercise fully the deep affections as motives. To be moved by the love of God requires engagement with the principalities and powers.

A powerful affirmation of this is the high-priestly prayer of Jesus from John's gospel. In addressing the first Person of the Trinity he says, ''I do not pray that thou shouldst take them out of the world, but that thou shouldst keep them from the evil one.''[3] Those who count themselves his flock must all face the prospect of praying in the world's wildfire and doublemindedness. ''Other-worldly'' conceptions of prayer will not disappear because of this. But soon or late, even those who hold to prayer principally as a ''heavenly telephone line'' realize that their own human substance must be engaged.

The extent to which true self-knowledge is given in prayer is a good measure, though not the only measure, of its adequacy to God. Of course, prayer is not self-analysis, a mere psychological help, or even a therapeutic ecstasy. Yet, in prayer, knowledge of God and knowledge of the self are correlated. This is an unmistakable conclusion of our explorations. Theological thinking which takes seriously the link between prayer and the affections is brought to a focus on this point. Praying is a way of being.

A way of being involves more than feeling, more than thinking, and more than doing. Popular religious interpretations of prayer try always to fit prayer into one or the other of these molds. Thus, we have prayer as mystical feeling, prayer as direct knowledge of God, or prayer as action in the world. These three misunderstandings must be countered.

With respect to prayer as feeling, Anthony Bloom's remark is apt:

> In our struggle for prayer the emotions (sic) are almost irrelevant; what we must bring to God is a complete, firm determination to be faithful to him and strive that God should live in us. We must remember that the fruits of prayer are not this or that emotional state, but a deep change in the whole of our personality. This is the principle of the heart which allows the whole being to stand before God. Such resolve to be ''before God'' is deeper than a sheer act of the will. It cannot occur unless we are also attuned to the presence of God in the world, and receptive to God's Word.
>
> As for prayer as special direct knowledge of God, the temptations are many. The quest for certainty and security in a time of anxiety and confusion always forces prayer toward the need for blessed assurance. There is, of course, assurance in faith.''[5]

But the development of private prayer as a special way of knowing God's will soon goes over to prayer as guaranteed assurance - as special ''gnosis'' or supernatural knowledge. Charles Williams rightly proposed the early church's corrective: ''See, understand, enjoy, said the Gnostic;

repent, believe, love, said the Church, and if you see anything, say so."[6] Prayer does illuminate and evoke knowledge of God, but only so far as this is part of our continual dwelling in God's Word.

In our age, the tendency is to define prayer primarily by its effects, or by our own consequent actions in the world. There is a partial truth in these contemporary views. Though it can never be reduced to its effects, prayer is indeed most clearly known by its fruits among those who pray. But when prayer becomes a special device or getting things done, such a conception is not far from "magic." Particularly in American life where stress is laid upon pragmatic efficiency and getting things done, we are most prone to this misunderstanding. A one-sided concern for the effectiveness of prayer leads, in Urban Holmes' phrase, to a spirituality of "prayer as production."[7]

Bearing these misunderstandings in mind, we can nevertheless stress the connection between prayer and its fruits. Praying occurs in the world of human intention and actions, the area of everyday life. The question is *not,* "Am I feeling better?" or "Do I really enjoy my prayer life?" but rather, "Is the will of God being realized in my life and in the life of the community?"

Beyond this sense of growing into and doing the will of God, a broader domain of prayer as being-in-the-world opens up. The will of God —whether in doing justice, giving the cup of cold water in Christ's name, or striving for peace —always meets with resistance in this world. Because of this we cannot rely on our own well-being as a test of the adequacy of our prayer. This was Jonathan Edwards' point in defining the distinguishing holy affections as the practical exercises of true virtue. Friendship consists in affection, but that which actually carries friends through fire and water for each other is the clearest sign of true affection. So also, friendship with God.

But we are not able, even in the most strenuous prayer life, to make the will of God work in the world without resistance and disappointment. Our intentions and actions in the name of God do not always see success. We must learn, as Bloom says, "That doing is not enough because we must not be drilled into christianity, but we must *become* christians."[8] So prayer is also a "not doing," a noninstrumental way of being in the world.

The world of human affairs is the theater of God's activity. If our faith is biblical, we profess this. Not only is the created order given as a good gift, it remains the realm of the divine creating, redeeming, and sanctifying power. Despite our attempts to avoid the world's complexity and heartbreak, we are called to worship and serve God there. We cannot expect a rose garden where the "dew is still on the roses," but shipwreck and rescue, cross and resurrection. Any deep recovery of Christian prayer will bring this with it. True intercession is impossible without it.

We are in the midst of one of those periods of quickening which, from time to time, the Church experiences along its pilgrimage. At its heart is the quest of the laity for learning and reality in prayer. Though it includes the renewal which emerges from reforms of the liturgy, this quickening is not simply the consequence of such intentional reforms. Underneath much that is superficial is the quest for prayer as a way of being Christian in the world. In some quarters the renewal of prayer has spawned the misunderstandings we have just mentioned. At the same time, it has also begun to reappropriate a more mature vision linking the fruits of prayer to the intensified presence of God in the world.

Some have regarded this quickening of prayer as simply a rebirth of the older pietisms. Some are convinced that Protestant enthusiasm has already infected Roman Catholicism, especially in ecumenically open sectors of American church life. For some it is the left-wing Reformation come home to roost. New charismatics and old schismatics seem in league, or in unholy wedlock.

Others find in the renewal of the spiritual life a simple, sociologically explainable reaction to change and complexity, and particularly a reaction to the excessive zeal for social and political gospels of the recent past. The "retreat inward," the escape to interiority, or the religious version of a "new narcissism"—all these are seen as signs of the times. Unfortunately, such sightings are accurate in many areas of church life. It is fashionable in some quarters to advertise: "the adventure of prayer—more rewarding, more exciting, bringing a lift to your life." This kind of rhetoric is a dead giveaway. The self-preoccupations implied by it are obvious. The bumper-sticker adventure of prayer is not a search for roots, but only for the first consolations of prayer. This, as the next chapter shows, is a final ironic misunderstanding of the role of the Christian affections in prayer.

Prayer can be a turning away from being present to the world's bewilderment and brokenness. There is always ambiguity in the renewed zeal for spirituality. There is no guarantee of emotional and spiritual depth. As someone once remarked, "There is much less here than meets the eye."

But something more is here. There is a convergence of interest from among laity and clergy alike. By virtue of baptism our primary vocation is prayer and service to God. The whole Church, not just the clergy or the pious elite, must follow a way, a truth, and a life. The heart of all discipleship in the world is learning again and again to pray. Understanding the sense and truth of prayer is foundational to being and doing God's Word and will. In our best moments, we know this. We turn, then to consider prayer as a response to the world's field of power and conflicting passions, and finally, to the tensions in living prayer as a way of being in the world.

Earlier I explored the question of how we "mean" our prayers. Let us ask that question in a new key. How can we both mean what we pray and pray what we mean in the world? But first, a prior question: To what is prayer a response?

The textbook answer to the last question is simple. Prayer is a response to the divine initiative, a response to God who calls us into praise and service, to communion, dialogue, and into the divine life which is fellowship with God. But I suspect that for most of us today who raise the question, the textbook answer is not the one which engages us first. The beginning point for much of us is that prayer is a response to human needs. It is a response to those features of our personal and social lives which "get to us" — which affect us. The rudimentary forms of prayer that have intensity and meaning for many people are elemental cries in the face of human need.

A plane falls out of the sky in New Hope, Georgia. It tries to land in a narrow street. A few feet more width between buildings and trees, and perhaps a few more would have lived. The plane crashes and a friend of mine cries, "No! God why is this happening!" — an unmistakable expression of deep and immediate feeling. This is a form of prayer which has intensity. It is a cry wrung from the heart. It is, I suspect, a clear case for most people of "meaning what is prayed."

If we are concerned with emotion, then surely, the experience of prayer in desperation cannot be ignored. Prayers which are wrung from us as cries in the face of sudden death, suffering, or injustice have reality. Such occasions present an image of "meaning what we pray" as feeling strongly, as being overwhelmed by the world's forces. If our basic model of meaningful prayer is of this sort, then what can we say about the forms lacking such intensity?

We must say unequivocally that Christian prayer does indeed respond to a broken and often inexplicable world. The beginnings of a certain kind of prayer are in such experiences. But in order for them to be integral to a life of prayer, the world must already be regarded in light of particular stories about it. Christian prayer beholds a world in the light of a particular story — told, enacted, and pondered in Scripture, proclamation and corporate prayer.

It is linked both to the raw needs of conflict and collision in existence, and to the world beheld as the arena of God's creating and redeeming love. Such a way of seeing and responding is articulated and made accessible in the multiple forms of the Word.

The question is not primarily, "To what does prayer respond?" but "To whom?" Christian prayer responds to a world known most fully in and through the judgment and mercy of God in Jesus Christ. The cries for justice and mercy, for release from bondage and for peace, see the fallen state of things.

We so easily assume that we *really* mean what we utter in prayer when it is solely a matter of our honesty and our convictions in the face of raw need. Our meaning appears so clear to us then, because our emotions are so close to the surface of the language. But we may be easily deceived here. Immediacy of feeling is not the same thing as emotional depth. One of the problems we face, psychologically and sociologically, with the new quest for prayer, is the continual confusion of those two things: intensity of feeling and emotional depth. Distinguishing them can be a delicate matter, since for many the renewal of prayer has been precisely a recovery of affection and feeling. We do not mean to deny this. Many Roman Catholics, for example, are coming out from under a non-affective form of praying which has been primarily experienced as obligation. For them, meaning in prayer has been rediscovered by virtue of the liveliness and the vitality of affections and feelings. My point is not to rule out such experiences, but to suggest something more sustained. However one may renew the face of prayer by virtue of discovering the affections, prayer will not be sustained with any depth and reality unless it forms us in deep emotions ingredient in the Christian story. Gratitude, joy, and patterns of repentance, compassion and forgiveness are such emotions.

As with the onset of great grief or gladness, the initial experiences of these emotions lack comprehension because of focal intensity. What the grief or gladness amounts to can only be shown once immediacy is past. It is easy to mistake the adrenal glands for the dispositions. The dispositions of the heart may remain untouched and untutored by Christ, while the feelings may be intense but directionless. We differ in our capacities to "feel," but we are equal with respect to our capacity for the deep emotions which true faith and lively praying forms and expresses.

The issue is whether we can pray what we mean and mean what we pray without being drawn into the way in which God views things. Our own enthusiasms are changed with the direction of our view. The meaning of prayer is not simply a matter of words. To pray is to become a living text. In this sense, meaning what we pray requires more than the onset of lively affections (though blessed are they who have lively affections who had none before and for whom "obligation" is being transformed). This harkens back to an earlier point — meaning what we pray requires that we share the form of life that goes with praying. Finding out what we mean when we pray may be more like discovering our loves, our fears, our joys, and the things over which we will weep together, than it is interpreting texts or doctrines. This discovery of loves and joys is much more than isolating the feelings produced in us.

When do you say and *mean* "Thank you"? Sometimes we say the words without much feeling. A dear friend will remind us, "Once more with feeling please." Then we may, in fact, say it with a little more affection. But the test of the kind of gratitude inherent in the Christian story is not measured by the one-time episode. Rather, over a long period of giving and receiving, losing and finding, of misunderstanding and being understood we can say, "How much 'thank you' has come to mean. My sense of gratitude has been constant in all these things, and I did not know it." This is an utterance which is far more than words. It becomes access to truth, a way of being formed in the language of gratitude which goes beyond "saying it with feeling." A lifetime's learning to grow in grace may be required to catch all it means to say, "Blessed art Thou, O Lord and God."

Again I must refer to St. Paul's manner of commending the Thessalonians to a Christian way of life. He lists the things which prevent life in Christ. They are familiar to us all. We are to abstain from evil in all of its forms, put away revenge, malice, and vices of earthly passions. In effect, he is saying, "Do away with those dispositions in your life and put on mutual respect and love — the virtues." In the midst of this, he calls upon the people of the church to "rejoice always, pray constantly, give thanks in all circumstances for this is the will of God in Christ Jesus for you." Even in the midst of all circumstances he commands the emotion of joy. Joy is not the kind of affection someone can simply "work up" as a matter of feeling. In circumstances of suffering, there must be a deeper joy in the heart than the "joy" of general well-being.

Prayer in St. Paul's writing begins in gratitude and recognizes God's presence shown to those who pray, regardless of circumstance. It is constant, in season and out of season, and the constancy of its object is God's steadfastness. Prayer is giving oneself to the Christian story in such a way that the emotions that characterize that life become the virtues exercised in concrete circumstances. This allows for the fact that prayer is, on occasion, dry and "meaningless." We do in fact lose sight of the story, and its presence may be in eclipse for periods in our life. Such a lack of meaning cannot be overcome by cultivating feeling apart from recovering the depth sense of the story. When the fires of affection burn low, we learn again to wait patiently, to listen for the Word, to watch in obedience.

Praying requires living in light of the Christian story in such a way that one can rejoice in God, whatever the circumstance, and continue in thanksgiving. To pray constantly is to be disposed before the face of God, in conspectu Dei. Prayer is not a mere aid to the living of a religious life. It is not an external goad or motivational technique. It is inseparable from having a life formed in joy, humility, gratitude, and compassion. These capacities are directed not only toward God, but toward all God's creatures. We respond to the world and all therein because we behold the world before the face of God.

If our prayer life is to be a genuine response, it will not be quickened by adapting new techniques for affectivity. Rather, the quickening will come in part because we recover a mode of meditation on the Word, and a heightened awareness and participation in various liturgical prayer-actions. Let us turn to a specific mode of prayer-action, the intercessions.

The restoration and renewal of the *Prayers of the People* (general intercessions) is having a profound impact upon clergy and laity alike. Here the laity discover that they can pray for others not vicariously through the clergy, but as their own gesture born out of the focus of our worship. Christ is in our midst praying with us and for us. Here is an explicit mode of corporate prayer in which the action is the engagement with the needs of the world in response to the divine identification with the lowly, the suffering, and the forsaken. The prayers of the faithful declare "Yes" to God in Christ, and provide an opening into God's identification with all humanity however fallen. Here we have a specific place of formation of our identity as intercessors — the identity Christ has for us. This is essential to response since Christ gives himself to us in the liturgy of Word and Sacraments. Our perceptions of his presence must never be disassociated from our neighbor and all in need. How can we forget our brothers and sisters *here* of all places, in the presence of his body and blood, and his Word — sung, prayed and proclaimed? To recognize the presence of Christ in Word and Eucharist is to confess his presence in the hurt and suffering of the neighbor as well. The former discloses the latter. In this sense, recovery of intercessory prayer is at the heart of the matter. The link between this action in the liturgy and a crucial aspect of spirituality is undeniable.

These things should characterize our intercessions: As Christ had compassion, so must we; as he encountered the brokenness of his children, so must we; as he loved, even in the face of death, so must we. In these ways we are being formed, not simply in the rhetoric of the text, but in living the text. It is here that our prayers for others may clearly manifest Christ. And their reality and meaning is always twofold, *toward* those in need, those whom God in Christ loves; and always *with* Jesus, our brother, who prays in our midst — Jesus, the intercessor, the mediator and high priest — with and through his people praying for all. The intercessions are the practice and the exercise of *being turned* so that we look in the direction that God's love is looking, and that means characteristically away from self, and away from the Church's inhouse preoccupation.

Four features of intercessory prayer need recovery. They are implied in what has already been said. First, we encounter new aspects and dimensions of ourselves as praying with others. Prayer for the early Church was never an isolated act. The notion of "closet" prayer, the interior prayer, or the prayer of the purified heart is what is desired, not merely the outward behavior. But for the early Church, praying was always praying in community, even when it was prayer alone. The distinction between individualistic devotional prayer and common prayer is foreign to the earliest periods of the Church.[9] This conception of prayer requires a truthfulness about who we are in relation to others as well as a new vulnerability which is very difficult to open up. There are communities of prayer where the vulnerability has simply been too much of the wrong kind. Spiritual pulse-taking should never substitute for the real vulnerability to one another and the world. The encounter with aspects of the self as praying with others is absolutely essential.

Secondly, only in and through solidarity with those in need can we begin to mean what we pray when we intercede. Only when we exercise the human capacity for empathy and solidarity with those for whom we pray, can our prayers grow in maturity. Praying for others openly and simply, surprises us with new dimensions of what it means to be in solidarity. We intend to be in solidarity with those who are affected by our ministry, which is a difficult thing. The meaning of these prayers, therefore, is not so much a matter of the style of praying but a matter of how we are disposed.

Thirdly, there is to be a recovery of intentionality in addressing the world's need to God. This means that in order to pray, we cannot simply "enjoy" better forms of intercession; we must learn, outside the rooms of prayer, the reality of commending others to God. The intentionality must be to commend all to God's love and mercy — as it were, to enter the heart of God. The intercessions must be texted and enacted as to provide a time for "letting be" for God. It is an action with an intentionality that matures over time and circumstance as we learn to address the world's need to God. Perhaps the most difficult thing is that this forces us to trust God even beyond our own highest capacity for pity and compassion. To intercede is to be attentive to God's hidden ways with the world.

Finally, to interecede without allowing the ministries of the community to be shown and be visibly represented by persons is to render the prayers inadequate to their intent and object. "The community of the people of God," Karl Barth reminds us, "speaks to the world by the fact of its very existence as a community of prayer."[10] It serves the world and speaks "by the simple fact that it prays for the world."[11] Karl Rahner, in a different context, takes up the theme of what a community of intercession must be when he contends that "the Church is the abiding presence of that primal sacramental word of definitive grace which is Christ in the world, effecting what is uttered by uttering it in sign."[12] I do not mean to make easy peace between an evangelical stress on the word of God and a more sacramental stress on the Church as *sacramentum,* or sign. Rather, both points remind us of the necessity of reflection upon the theological substance of being a community of interecession. We make manifest the reason for our praying for the world: Christ precedes us, and will be encountered in the hurt and needy. Has he not said it will be so? Where encountering the reality of human need is *not* part of our experience in intercessory prayer, no amount of lovely text — said or sung — will suffice.

Prayer is a worldly activity in the sense we have uncovered. It is indeed a response to the world by virtue of being a response to the divine initiative, Word in flesh. Intercessory forms of prayer force us to recognize that our faith must be lived in the world of power and conflicting passions. These basic considerations lead us finally to the problem of the permanent tensions which characterize prayer as being in the world.

Some may say that in our age and cultural circumstances prayer as praise and adoration of God in heaven has shifted, or is being transformed, to prayer as love of neighbor and to the effects of prayer in the human sphere. Putting the issue this way raises concretely the perennial tension between prayer and action in the Christian life. This is often thought to be the same as the tension between contemplation and action.

Two points must be made immediately. First, the stress on love of neighbor should not be regarded as entailing the necessary diminishment of the love of God. Such a view seems to place love of God and love of neighbor on either side of a balancing scale. The Lord's commandment, as we noted in chapter four, is not to be taken this way. Jesus did not intend to put these in some kind of inverse ratio to one another.

Secondly, we should not assume that the tension between prayer and action is to be equated with the contrast between contemplation and action. This identifies prayer completely with "contemplative prayer." Would it not be far more illuminating to speak of contemplative dimensions of all genuine Christian prayer?

Beyond these two points, however, lies yet the most decisive consideration. Tensions are built into the Christian life itself because they are built into the very concept of praying and the call to holiness at the heart of the gospel. This is the focal point of Christian existence: Christ's own life is one of active prayer and prayerful action. It is fitting to speak of his whole life as a prayer, a continual self-offering. In exploring what Christ's life signifies we are led to ponder anew the necessity of understanding prayer and action not in opposition, but in tension required by particular moments in that stream of life which seeks to grow into the full stature of Christ.

It is obvious that praying is itself one activity performed among other activities within the Christian life. Here is a natural contrast: now the community prays together, now we are engaged in the works of service and love. But this itself assumes a link between faith and works, between praying and the intentional actions which express the Christian's life in the world. Here we need the theology of that much abused epistle of James: "As the body apart from the spirit is dead, so faith apart from works is dead" (2:26). In light of our approach to the Christian affections, faith without works is not so much "dead" as it is self-preoccupied. Affections which do not become the wellspring and motive for action turn in upon themselves. Faith contemplating only itself leads to sickness.

There is a contrast between being and doing within the Christian life. But we also need a contrast between prayerful life and a life without prayer. These are complementary, not conflicting, contrasts. Thus we must consider the notion of the pervasiveness of prayer as a mark of Christian maturity. We must extend the concept of prayer from its application to specific acts of worship (of verbal prayer or silent recollections) to its application over the whole of one's life. As Origen and others have said, the whole of the life of a saint is one continuous prayer.[13] We must begin with praying in an ordinary sense of a specific religious act, and move to a sense of prayer which covers the whole life of faith, seeking to "pray constantly" in the Pauline phrase.

Thus we can say that prayer is "useless" — it is also a *not doing*.[14]
Here we highlight its non-instrumental character. This point emerged in our
earlier discussion of the "fruits" of prayer. Christian prayer is not
undertaken solely in order to accomplish this or that. Simply put, it is a
response to what we are called to be. We are to attend to God and to God's
Word and be moved with the promptings of divine justice, mercy and
compassion. It is a dialogue of the affections, the Word written into our
hearts.

"The glory of God is the living man."[15] Thus St. Irenaeus asserted
once and for all against the future heresies a fundamental truth we must
rediscover in our approach to prayer. The life of human beings is also the
living relation to God.

Now we see why contemplation as such cannot be the privileged basis
of Christian prayer. It may certainly precede being alive in the world, or it
may follow a given period of strenuous service. The chronology is not the
point. Rather, we must say that neither contemplation nor action are the
basis. If we are correct, there is something deeper than both, namely the
continuing relationship and dialogue between the whole of the self and God,
and between the whole life of the Church and the Realm of God. In this sense
we claim that the prayer of Jesus was not any single utterance, or period of
withdrawal, but his whole life. It was offered in the obedience, a sacrifice
acceptable to God.

Explicit periods of prayer may need to be contemplative as such. But ·
explicit prayer is not isolated from the whole of what it is to exist in the
world. Christian prayer is to be "in spirit and in truth," as Jesus told the
Samaritan woman. To be so is not a matter of contemplation or action; it
is the Spirit's own praying which breathes into all our doings and prayings.
Christian prayer in the world is in relation to "everything" and "in all
circumstances" and "at all times in the Spirit." The contemplative aspect
of all Christian prayer is not in opposition to prayer as action. The
contemplative and active dimensions complement and complete one another. As in the deep affections there is both receptivity and an active
movement toward the objects of various emotions, so there is necessarily a
passive and an active movement in the heart of the person praying.

Prayer in each of its modes — praise, confession, silent petition,
intercession, adoration, and thanksgiving — manifests this double movement. It is not that praise is active while silence is pure passivity. Even in
praise the contemplative dimension must be present in the absorption of the
Word. In thanksgiving, the recital of God's mighty acts must be recalled and

pondered in the mind of the Church if thanksgiving is to be fully expressive of faith. Likewise in silent recollection there is an active yearning toward God, and an attentive focused stand before the mystery of grace.

In these ways, contemplative and active rhythms are the systole and diastole of all Christian prayer. Contemplation is not pure vision and enjoyment, while action is hearing and serving in the stream of life. Within Christianity, Jesus' own role as the servant of all shows that the ordinary life of being in the world — family, politics, cultural energies — is part of the prayer-action of Christ.

Thus we cannot oppose the joy of contemplating heavenly things and the grim courage of active mission in the world. Both contain a joy which flows forth from having one's affections fixed upon the excellency and beauty of God's redeeming love.

Prayer must show forth this proper tension, for the stream of events and experience which comprises human action often works against the movement of attentiveness to the Word. It is difficult to behold the things of heaven in the midst of preoccupations and distraction. Thus no theological theory about the preoccupations and distraction. Thus no theological theory about the action/contemplation polarity can resolve the concrete problems of struggling to create a climate of prayer and receptiveness in our busy lives. In this sense, no matter how much we can speak of our whole life as a praying, we must still exercise explicit times of prayer in community and alone.

Here then is the paradox: only in the conscious activity of praying do we find the conditions for receiving the shared life of God as a gift. As Jacques Ellul observes, "it is prayer which creates the silence needed for prayer."[16] But this activity is not simply another "act" alongside all the others; it opens out upon the capacity for any action whatever. In order to gain this "not acting" we must be attuned to Scripture and to silence. Contemporary life in the world with its burdened conscience and busyness often turns us away from prayer as a "natural," or innate, gesture of the self. lacking the desire to pray or not seeing the point, we may look for some special "peak experience" to take its place. But we must learn again that Word and silence form the matrix of prayer, both contemplative and active. As Henry Nouwen puts it: "The word of God draws us into silence; silence makes us attentive to God's word. The word of God penetrates through the thick of human verbosity to the silent center of our heart; silence opens in us the space where the world can be heard."[17]

Prayer is congruent with the *human* character of divine revelation. The divine self-communication does not destroy the world in coming to it. Likewise the Word of God does not destroy or reduce our humanity in being received. Rather, the Word addresses us as a call to our full humanity. This is why the giving of oneself to God's Word is intimately linked with prayer as self-offering. Seeking God can so easily take the form of a kind of disembodiment, a spiritual withdrawal from the world. But this is both a withdrawal from the self in which the Word is to be rooted and a withdrawal from the fulness of God's self-giving. The whole of our life is to be offered and the whole of God's self-giving is to be received. These movements are not contradictory, but are part of the life-giving tension in all true Christian prayer.

The fruits of the Spirit in our life are always embodied and can never adequately be kept as private consolation. The deep affections of thanksgiving, joy, and gratitude constitute the continual prayer over time, the continual dialogue with God. "The awareness in prayer of the work of the Spirit in the world binds the person who is praying more closely to the human activities of the transformation of the universe, where the groaning of the Spirit can be perceived."[18] Knowing God requires worldly embodiment. The gifts of the Spirit are bestowed as capacities to know and to recognize God everywhere, even God's hidden glory in the groaning of creation for its liberation.

The otherness of grace is not an alien phenomenon in human persons who struggle to pray. Holiness-and-godliness is indeed a gift which violates what we were intended to be in this world. To be "born anew" is to come into new dispositions in one's own, not someone else's life. Yet one is no longer governed by the world's ways. The working of the Spirit cannot be confined to the "interior" of our life. The gifts and graces are for existence in the human field of forces. Even the work of the Holy Spirit may be said to be worldly in this sense.

But the secret hidden from the eyes of the world which animates our being in the world lies more deeply still. Prayer responds to the world of suffering and dense ambiguity. Its animating life is both hidden from the plain view and not contained by the highest ecstasy. The Word and Spirit of God come in forms comparable with our being human. Our humanity is not reduced or evacuated into "pure spirit." Rather, it is in the process of transformation, sanctification and glorification by the Creator to whom we are returning. Thus as von Balthasar rightly claims, "The tensions inherent in human nature are shared by revelation and assumed by God himself in his union with mankind.''[19]

The words still can pray:

Because the Holy Ghost over the bent
World broods with warm breast and with ah! bright wings.[20]

seven
Praying With Christ:
Signs of Living Prayer

> For this reason I bow my knees before the Father, from whom every
> family in heaven and on earth is named, that according to the riches of his
> glory he may grant you to be strengthened with might through his Spirit
> in the inner man, and that Christ may dwell in your hearts through faith;
> that you, being rooted and grounded in love, may have power to
> comprehend with all the saints which is the breadth and length and height
> and depth, and to know the love of Christ which surpasses knowledge, that
> you may be filled with all the fullness of old. (Ephesians 3:14-19)

For its comprehensiveness and luminosity few passages in Scripture
rival this ardent prayer for the life and ministry of the Church. It presents a
living image of the shape and character of Christian life to which the whole
people of God is called. Such heightened vision of the vocation of the entire
household of God sheds light upon that household's various ministries. The
letter to the church at Ephesus makes clear the focus of all affections and
actions in Christ. Whatever variety of gifts for ministry have been bestowed,
they are knit together and given their fundamental *telos* by the stature of the
fullness of Christ, into whom "we are to grow up in every way." Learning
Christ in his fullness is not something the Christian community could
choose to do; rather, it is the indelible character of the hope to which we have
been called. Not to be thus formed is to miss the reality of the Christian
vocation, bestowed by baptism into Christ.

One of the greatest defects within American churches today is the lack
of focused spirituality *in* and *through* our ministries. Parish priests and
pastors are pushed and pulled in many different directions, and are subject
to a bewildering variety of demands. Lay persons search in vain for a
defining center in the church's life. Images of success and failure current

87

in the churches to which we acquiesce are often in conflict with the nature of Christian ministry itself. We know how easy it is to conform to the institutional, or anti-institutional, role given by the pragmatic ebb and flow of popular expectations and the routine of "managing" the church. It is equally tempting for some of us to embrace uncritically the rising tide of personalistic and sectarian pieties. In either case, we become spiritual dilettantes, or worse, "children, tossed to and fro and carried about with every wind of doctrine. . . ."

Unless ministries are shaped in the pattern of Christ and our lives are hid with him in God, all the activity and sincere piety in the world will not suffice for this "one thing most necessary." For how will we be able to show forth the ministry of Christ in the world unless we are formed into his life, passion, death, and resurrection — unless we comprehend in some way "the breadth and length and height and depth" of the love of God in Christ Jesus?

As I observed earlier, we are in the midst of one of those periods of quickening which, from time to time, the Church experiences along its journey. The awakening of interest in prayer and the spiritual life has generated popular books and articles, and innumerable cassettes. Various movements have been generated by concern for renewal of "religious experience," especially among the laity in Roman Catholic and Protestant traditions. The very word "spirituality" has become popular coinage - a word which has not been in the stock Protestant vocabulary until quite recently. Even theological seminaries have begun to see a "new problematic" which requires attention: new forms of spiritual formation.

Surely this new concern, whether its source is cultural or ecclesial, has an air of ambiguity about it. New enthusiasm for prayer and the inner life often gives the impression of being the latest "fashion" in American religious life. As the sixties involved "relevance" and social-political gospels of one sort or another, so the seventies brought the "turning inward." Much is already being said in some quarters that the eighties brought about the "escape from social mission into piety," or the "new narcissism" in the culture at large, of which concern for prayer seems to some observers but an extension. It is undeniably true that prayer can be, as Jacques Ellul and others have reminded us, a dangerous deceit, full of human religiousness and spiritual illusion. Just because we live in a period of quickening is no guarantee that an authentic renewal of prayer grounded in a recovery of the Word of God is in the making.

There is, however, another aspect in the renewed concern for prayer and spirituality that signals more than the latest cultural response to the spirit of the age. A long-range process of reform and renewal arising within Christianity is taking place. As a result of challenges to religious and theological authority and truth, we have been thrown back upon the fundamental questions of identity and form of life in time and history. Easy assumptions about what it is to be Christian and to exercise ministry in the name and authority of Christ have been shattered. In attempting to live out a profound sense of *semper reformanda,* various Christian communions have found that our inherited conceptions of holiness and discipleship have been in transition along with our inherited patterns of worship. The pain of fundamental questions has given a character of depth and urgency to the relation between Christian prayer and our ministries. For this we may be grateful: that the Holy Spirit is at work still in our turmoil and in our struggle to pray. "Likewise the Spirit helps us in our weakness; for we do not know how to pray as we ought . . ." (Romans 8:26). "Professional competence" is not enough, nor is sincere but comfortable membership.

I invite you, therefore, to ponder and to receive again what we already know: *"We are called to be living reminders of Jesus Christ, and to manifest the mystery of the Church's life before God in this world. We are to be signs of living prayer.*[1] Christian ministry — both lay and clerical — cannot claim its own authenticity or power unless it "grow up in every way into him who is the head . . .from whom the whole body, joined and knit together . . .when each part is working properly, makes bodily growth and upbuilds itself in love" (Ephesians 4:15-16).

The request basic to all Christian life and ministry is still, "Lord, teach us to pray." This request indicates a readiness to follow the life and truth of Jesus as Lord. When fully explored, and not simply taken for granted, the answer to such a request encompasses the entire Christian life. For Christian prayer cannot be entered into without entering into the Word of God in fullness. To hear and to assimilate this Word in its fullness is to enter into the very life of the Word made flesh. From the outset, we know that more is involved in spirituality than the learning of various techniques for prayer. And it is far more than learning *about* prayer, or *about* "ascetical" or "mystical" theology. To pray is to dwell with the Word.

There are two great dissociations which stand in our way. Most Christians in our culture inherit a legacy of separation between liturgy and personal faith on the one hand; and, on the other, a separation between theology and prayer. Neither of these dissociations are peculiar to Protestantism, (see, for example, the strong discussion of this point in Louis Bouyer's *Liturgical Piety*) but they take root readily in American Protestant soil. Generations of people have been brought up to understand common worship primarily as "external and outward forms" belonging to the public rituals of the Church. All too frequently liturgy is regarded as an outward and visible ceremonial whose primary function is to arouse and sustain "inner" personal faith. The rites and prayers of liturgical worship still strike many as only accidentally or externally related to real piety which is private and inward.

With respect to the second dissociation, many clergy are trained in theology in a way which has little or no direct relation to the shape and exercise of their personal faith. Theology seems to many a kind of "special language" which a seminary or academic environment requires us to speak, but which has no direct bearing upon the first-order language of faith we must speak in preaching, praying, counselling, teaching, and exhortation. Many a bright young seminarian preaches "theologically" as though reading an academic treatise. In sum, the inner connection between theology and prayer seems distant and remote. Such an attitude betrays the impoverishment of the Word as source of theological reflection and the formation and expression of our piety. This is true for clergy and laity alike.

But the pattern of life given in Christ as the Word of God is both individual and communal. It is, on the one hand, rooted in the particularity of each individual's life brought to focus in confessing Jesus as Lord. On the other hand, that very confession of faith and trust (and the way of being in the world) is sustained by the communal memories, sign-actions and continuing prayer of the body of the faithful. The self-communication of God-with-us is continuous with the pattern given in Scripture; yet it is freshly understood in every age precisely through the ongoing prayer and life of the Church. Such prayer and dwelling with the Word can never be self-enclosed, since a living tradition is constantly returning to its own sources: this is the *semper reformanda*. Aberrations and one-sided development in piety and in theology occur whenever persons are not formed in both the communal and individual dimensions of that pattern of life. This history of Western spirituality illustrates both the Protestant tendency toward individualism and excessive subjectivism, and the Catholic tendencies toward collectivism and excessive objectivism in faith. Neither form of life is fully receptive to the deepest reaches of the Word.

As Hans Urs von Balthasar has so beautifully put the point:

> The first danger is that of Protestantism, which has such a vivid sense of Revelation in the Word as such, and is ceaselessly occupied with it.

This concern is certainly to be admired and imitated by . . .Catholics; yet it often lacks something which would allow the study of the Word of God to develop into true contemplation and vision. It overlooks the essential indwelling of the Word in the Eucharist and in the Church as in the mystical body and vine; with the result that this concern with the revealed Word cannot be said to resemble Mary's.

Catholics, on the other hand, fall short - not indeed as a matter of principle, but often to practice - of a like perseverance in hearing the Word. They confine themselves to the actual possession of grace as assured to them by the Church and the sacraments; and in fact, the best contemplative tradition often tends to modulate from hearing to a tranquil seeing, from submissive reception to spiritual possession (as "wisdom" and the "gift of the Holy Ghost"). The Catholic tradition of contemplation must recapture the element adopted by Protestantism as its watchword and standard."[2]

Even the most cursory examination of the life into which we ought to be formed reveals its dual character: both individual and communal, devotional and liturgical, contemplative and active. To pray with Jesus is to enter his whole life in the Trinity: the second Person listening to the first, a constant dialogue between the first and second, animated by the third. The only way in which we may address dissociation of liturgy and theology from personal faith and prayer is by entering fully into the form of life shown in Jesus Christ as the Word of God. Entering fully into the communal prayer of the Church requires our being shaped in a pattern of deep emotions and dispositions. If our prayer is to be a listening and a dialogue with God, as Jesus teaches us by his praying and being, then we must enter into the way in which the "heart" is formed. Prayer, whether liturgical or devotional, is far more than keeping the words in a certain order, or reciting the "correct" theology: it is a continual process of orienting and being oriented to life. The deepest features of human desire, thought, emotion, and will are re-oriented and continually in dialogue with the Word. Theology must reflect on the question of the relationship between the Word, which is focused in Jesus Christ, and the religious affections.

It is clear for any who undertake the life of prayer that meaning what one prays cannot be cultivated simply by force of will. Nor can it be gained by a firm intellectual grasp of the relevant doctrines alone. To mean what one prays is part of living out the teachings and living through the deeper emotions patterned by the language of Scripture and prayer. Yet here is precisely where a misunderstanding arises. This living out of certain emotions is not to be construed primarily as having intense feelings or experiences. The capacity to mean what one prays has less to do with intensity of "feelings" caused or generated as it has to do with the genuineness, perdurability, and depth of emotion inhering in the way of life which is taken up. As C.S. Lewis observed, "Emotional intensity is itself no proof of spiritual depth. If we pray in terror, we shall pray earnestly; it only proves that terror is an earnest emotion. Only God. . .can let the bucket down to the depths in us."[3]

The natural assumption is to connect "really meaning" the language of prayer with "feeling it now," or more generally with summoning a special honesty and sincerity. "Meaning what we say" appears so clear to us when in fact our affections are running high, and we are felt so close to the surface of our utterances. But this may be a deception. Immediacy of feeling is not the same as emotional depth. At the same time, unless what we say issues forth in some form of experienced conviction and/or consolation at some points in the prayer life, we are most likely to diminish our discernment of prayer as revelatory. At worst, praying itself becomes a matter of empty repetition of formulaic language.

Intensity of feeling and emotional depth and range are not the same. This is a delicate matter, since many Christians have come out from under an obligatory, non-affective view of prayer. For many, the renewal of prayer has been a recovery of vivid affection and feeling. Meaning in prayer (as well as the "meaning of prayer") has been rediscovered by virtue of sudden vitality of experience and freedom for, as we say, "being emotional." One must rule out such experiences; yet a substantial point must be made. However one may renew the face of prayer by virtue of discovering affectivity, the intrinsic connection between praying and being will not be sustained unless we come to be formed in the deep emotions which are ingredient in the Christian story itself; gratitude, joy, awe, repentance, loving-kindness, and compassion.

The issue is whether we pray what we mean and mean what we pray as Christians without being drawn into the way in which God views the world. Our own enthusiasms are tempered and even radically changed with the direction of our regard. This means that the meaning of prayer is not simply a matter of honest words uttered honestly. The language of love opens access to truth (or falsehood). A lifetime's learning to grow in love may be required to catch the deeper echo of what it means to experience the range of human loves. How much more is the love ingredient in the Christian story measured, not by episodic intensities but by steadfast love. The Psalmist continually sings: "For God's steadfast love endures forever."

From such a recognition, intense affectivity may flow; and, upon occasion, from an experience of focused insight, the dispositions for more enduring love may be laid down in our life. That is, from an overwhelming experience of being mercifully loved and accepted, a person may find new capacities for steadfast love suddenly in place. Yet the holy affection of love, as Jonathan Edwards would point out, consists in the ongoing exercise of that love over time.

In the letter to the Thessalonians (I Thess. 5:16), St. Paul exhorts them to a Christian way of life. He first lists the things which prevent life in Christ. They are familiar; we are to avoid evil in all its forms, to put away revenge, malice, and the dark emotions and vices. We are to put on mutual respect and love. In the midst of the exhortation, he calls upon the people to "rejoice always, pray constantly, give thanks in all circumstances." He commands the emotions of joy, gratitude and love. These are not the kinds of affections which can be simply worked up as a matter of feeling. For he calls forth a deeper joy which can abide all circumstances, good or ill. The constant prayer, of course, is not an incessant pouring forth of words about God and the affections; rather, it is a life lived prayerfully and with attention to those features of the Gospel for which one can be constantly grateful, and in which one can continually rejoice despite the rise and fall of all worldly enthusiasms.

Prayer here begins in gratitude, and its constancy, in season and out of season, is linked to the constancy of its object: God's love in Christ. "For God's love endures forever." This holds, I think, for all Christian prayer. It is a giving of oneself to the Christian story in such a way that there is an internal connection between the emotions and virtues exercised in that life and the meaning of what is prayed. Prayer will in fact be, on occasion, and perhaps for long periods, dry and "meaningless" in the popular sense of that term. And where affectivity is lacking, we may lose sight of the story, and its power and reach may be in eclipse for periods in our life. Such a lack of meaning cannot be overcome by cultivating feelings apart from recovering the depth of the story, and for allowing our lives to be qualified and be shaped by it. The "meaninglessness" referred to here must always be met with the admonition to "wait," to "listen," and to attend to the Word.

Thus praying requires living in light of the Christian mystery in such a way that we may rejoice whatever the circumstance and continue to praise. To pray constantly is to be disposed *in conspectu Dei*, before the face of God. It is not a motivating technique. Rather, prayer is part of having a life formed in joy, gratitude, awe, and compassion. These capacities (which we learn to call gifts when we understand them) are directed toward God and all

God's creatures. We respond to others because we behold them and the world before the face of God.

Thomas Merton has wisely observed:

> We should be deeply grateful when our prayer really brings us an increase of clear understanding and felt generosity and we should by no means despise the stimulation of sensible devotion when it helps us to do whatever we have to do, with greater humility, fidelity, and courage.[4]

In fact, we may add, these kindled affections and experienced consolations are to be expected. But we cannot stop there, for the journey of a prayerful life sometimes take us well beyond that point. Surely there is also prayer in face of the "absence" of God, and that which may lead to a kind of *apatheia,* perhaps antithetical to the having of affections. Here we must heed Merton's continuing line of reasoning:

> Emotional versatility is a help at the beginning of the interior life, but later on it may be an obstacle to progress. At the beginning, when our senses are easily attracted to created pleasure, our emotions will keep us from turning to God unless they themselves can be given some enjoyment and awareness of the value of prayer . . .But if our prayer always ends in sensible pleasure and interior consolation, we run the risk of resting in these things which are by no means the end of the journey.[5]

The issues suggested here are large and quite beyond development in these pages. But surely this point is a reminder that Christian prayer is also an eschatological gesture and utterance. Thus it cannot "contain" its object. Even what is given to the deep emotions by way of poetic understanding of God and the world is not fully given, not because God capriciously wishes only part of the divine life to be shared, but because our life here in pilgrimage is always partial, temporally situated, and "possessive." We can be reminded by such prayer that God is not wholly "experienceable." The cessation of all worldly affection serves to remind us that we live and pray "between the times." There is also the discipline of "absence" in prayer which leads to greater humility and self-knowledge. All this is to say that even the full flowering of the holy affections in this life is not the end of Christian prayer, though surely such flowering in our ministries is necessary to growth in the Spirit. The happy beholding of God and all God's works is both affective and noetic. But Christian prayer has also an *eschatological* tension and pervading its forms and its teleology which can never be ignored. We already participate in the Reign of God, but not in its fullness until, in God's own time, it is bestowed upon the whole world. "Lord, teach us to pray." And he answers, as of old, "Our Father." In the words Jesus gives us, we find an inexhaustible source for every generation's struggle to pray, because these are not merely a form of words — they present a form of life. We can rediscover prayer only by discovering the life that goes with it. We learn again how to pray only from one whose life and teaching reveal what it is to be prayerful, to offer the whole self as one's "spiritual worship." The mystery now and always will be that in learning to pray "Our Father," we deepen our discernment of Christ as Word of God and Son of Man.

In meditating on the "Our Father," we come into the language of address. We are to call God "Abba" as Jesus does. To call the Holy One of Israel, the Creator of heaven and earth, by this affectionate and intimate name is to render ourselves childlike and vulnerable. Yet this is the very point. In trust we dispose our whole life toward God and in so doing we find one another as God's children. Those who dare utter "Abba" are bound each to each in familial love. To pray "Our Father" is to express unity with others who so pray, and solidarity with the whole human family whom God judges and loves.

The link between saying and being, between praying and meaning, is begun at this profound utterance, "Holy be your name:" your name, O Lord, be made holy in us. We pray that the Name be glorified and made holy in us. But the utter holiness of God throws fierce light on our impurity and profaneness. Is it any wonder that we experience ambivalence toward such a One? Either we with Peter say, "Depart from me, for I am sinful," or we say, "Lord, to whom shall we go?" To flee or to be made pure: both responses are part of our meaning if praying is to reflect encounter with Jesus the Word. Here then, is the command of our Lord's prayer — to conjoin in our life both awe and adoration with the familial love of a child to mother and father. God's name will be made holy in us so far as we receive and manifest the life holiness requires, a simplicity and second naivete, if you will — a simplicity of mind and heart. In awe and love we continually pray that we be made signs just as Jesus is the fullest sign of the reality of God and the Realm of God to come.

"Your will be done" is a cry and a command; it wells up in our human distress under evil, and it is the word of God upon which we stand. So often praying is filled with requests for every human wish and want under heaven. Are we not taught what our needs and wishes are? Yes. The Alexandrian fathers were fond of the phrase, ''Ask for the great and spiritual gifts.'' Ask for God's own self-giving. In this way prayer is a continual refining of our wants and desires, a continual reminder of whose we are, for whom we shall live. That the Rule and Reign of God be found growing in our midst, that the work of reconciliation be shown in our lives, and the final triumph of God's reign be expected: *these* are the great things. But always in our experience of ''Your will be done'' is that terrifying and terrible strength of Jesus Christ in Gethsemane. ''Nevertheless, not my will be done.'' For in this world we both seek and undergo God's will. We live after the Fall and before the consummation. In learning to pray with Christ we are not told, ''Pray this, and things will work out.'' He was himself to be delivered into the hands of our evil, the complicities of our own ministry. But the Reign of God has broken in upon the darkness, and ''in thy will is our peace.''

''Give us today daily bread.'' We move from the great things to the everyday. We know that we shall not live by bread alone, yet we ask for the simple things, the small matters, the common, the ordinary — these are to be part of our praying, also. This is because the Lord who teaches us to pray came to share the concrete, narrow and limited aspects of our life, including the need to be sustained daily. So to ask for bread, we acknowledge dependency upon a source of life apart from our own strength. Is it not a great mystery that there is no opposition between earthly bread and spiritual bread? The holy one whose thoughts encompass all being is that heavenly One concerned to sustain us. So Jesus taught, so he lived, so we must pray. Jesus takes the ordinary, makes it extraordinary, sign and sacrament of his power, and he says of the bread at table, ''This is my body.'' When we pray this prayer, we join hands with all others at the Lord's table where he fills the hungry. We dare pray in a world of hunger and thirst. To receive life and daily bread from the hand of God is to be committed to feeding the hungry, for here the Lord is also.

''Forgive us our sins.'' We ask for bread and we ask for forgiveness, two undeniable, indelible human necessities. To knock, to seek, and to ask is not simply a private matter. When we ask that our sins be forgiven, we admit the deep connection between our life and the guilt of humankind. To persist in season and out in this prayer is continually to hold before God the incredible darkness in which humanity chooses to dwell. Because our hearts are defensive, and we find it difficult to confess faults, our hearts are hardened. No compassion or sympathy will dwell where there is no confession and no forgiveness. ''As we forgive others'' is not to be understood as ''the more I forgive, the more God will forgive.'' Forgiving brothers and sisters is not a bargaining point for God's mercy. Rather, in our praying, if there is no capacity to forgive in our lives, then we simply cannot understand what God has forgiven. To accept and forgive those who have wronged us is a condition for understanding what has been done for us, a condition for receiving reconciliation. Whenever we pray and wherever we offer gifts to God, we must be reconciled so that ''your father in heaven may forgive you your trespasses.'' So we dare lift up even hardness of heart.

''And deliver us from evil.'' Here we come full circle and start again with where we began. The cry of anguish in the midst of evil, suffering and darkness is taken up even into our Lord's life. Are we seriously to believe that God will prevent us from being tempted? ''Lead us not into temptation?'' Surely not. If we choose to follow the way, there will be temptations we will have of which those who do not follow will never dream. The saints have temptations we can barely imagine. Yet there is a promise that we shall not be tempted beyond our strength, and part of the power of the Lord's life in this prayer keeps the fact from becoming a religious cliche. So we are not to prove our faith in the face of suffering and evil as though we had to bear it ourselves. Rather, we are to proclaim and pray that Christ has won victory over all forms of temptation, except our individual spiritual pride which may render us defenseless before the Evil One. The final petition should be experienced as abrupt and harsh, for it recognizes the presence of evil in the very midst of our religiousness. It speaks of more than worldly temptations. It refers to the threat of the final trial which no follower of Jesus can be spared. At the time of the consummation, when the Reign shall come and God's holiness be fully revealed, we pray that we not succumb to the trial. In this petition as in all others, we are constantly formed in the mystery of Christ, continually maturing in the affections which go together with a life formed in the one with whom we pray.

So then, we respond to the world, suffering, dying, rejoicing, growing, sinning, and being blessed. But we respond to the world through the One in whom the world is truly seen — the One who always points us in the same direction the divine love looks. Thus, meaning what we pray and praying what we mean involves rediscovering the connection between liturgical participation and the shape of the Christian virtues and affections. Interiority is itself best nurtured by recovery of modes of mediation on both the actions and the texts. Here vitality and maturity are part and parcel of the intensification of the world, the intensification of the world and the self before God. If you and I are to be involved in a true recovery and deepening, and not merely a fashion or a trend, we cannot dissociate responding to the world from responding to these various presences of Christ in our common ministries. There are enough illustrations and deceits in the name of piety already abroad in our day. We do not need to compound the difficulty by making prayer a technique for being more virtuous; or by making it a therapeutic surrogate for what we do not intend to face in the midst of our life, particularly in the engagement and complicities of our own ministries. To pray constantly then is to make all occasions a thankful remembrance before God.

Finally, the link between individual prayer and the liturgy will become clearer if we uncover the kind of holiness which being in the world with Jesus requires. The deep emotions of gratitude, repentance, and joy, the virtues of humility, hope, and compassion in solidarity with all human beings, indeed with all creatures - these are the human realities which are the bloodstream of prayer. All these become the commonplaces for meaning what we pray and praying what we mean. We are to signify Christ to the world, even as Christ is given to us continually in our praying through him. At the heart of all Christian prayer is this living with the one mystery which is God's life embracing us into God. We pray with the incarnate Person revealed and revealing in a Word made flesh — a mystery still veiled from our eyes, but open to our ears and the gracious affections the Spirit bestows upon the heart.

We began by admitting a problem: the lack of theologically integral and sustaining spirituality in our ministries. We called to mind what our baptismal vocation is: to be living reminders of Jesus Christ, and to manifest the mystery of the Church's life before God in the world. But to *be* signs of living prayer requires the overcoming of our inherited dissociations between liturgy, theology, and personal piety. Only by recovering the Word in its plenitude as that in which we dwell, do we begin to ''comprehend'' with all the saints what is the breadth and length and height and depth, and to know the love of Christ which surpasses knowledge.

The Word of God in Scripture, and in the flesh, addresses and intensifies the whole of what we are, including all that is most inward in us. To pray is to dwell with Jesus Christ whose whole life offered is our prayer of thanksgiving, joy, repentance, and love — the fruits of his Spirit bestowed and embodied in our visible ministries offered with, in and through Jesus Christ our Lord.

Afterword

So much remains unsaid, in one sense, explorations can begin only now after this rough map has been drawn. Sketching the outlines of the territory, however, has revealed some of its striking yet neglected features.

The religious affections are pathways that invite further following. This book has not addressed some of the most pressing personal problems many now have with prayer. Nor has it attempted to resolve doubts arising from what are normally regarded ask the "emotional crises" of modern life — guilt, anxiety, anger, or boredom. Freud, Jung, and Erickson still wait in the wings to have their say. For the time being we have remained close to conceptual and theological clarification of relations between prayer and the religious affections. Yet such personal and practical problems require a new grasp of these relations if they are to be faced adequately, much less resolved. Our joys and griefs, hopes and fears, our sorrows and our gladness — these are precisely the points of access to God's way with human beings in the world. This is evident in history and in Scripture; it is so with each of us.

Because our existence is known most deeply and intimately through our emotions and passions, the place of encounter with God is in their midst. The theologically untutored heart has its story to tell. We must listen to such stories in ourselves and from our companions along the way. The heart schooled in the inhumanity of our age is racked with suffering and anguish. If we do not listen to it, praying will lack reality and point. Yet all these natural energies and sufferings which constitute our passional life are not, in and of themselves, capable of bringing us into dialogue and communion with the living God. There is no determinate form of religious faith unless such natural passions and capacities for emotion are given shape and expression by religious teachings in and through the language of worship.

But in our times the culture of self-fulfillment creates a peculiar set of difficulties. It is one thing to say that the very language of the liturgy and the struggle to live with a grateful heart are at root self-deceptive. Such reductionism is still all around, but we have begun to see this claim as a crude application of Freud or Marx. Closer to home is the fact that our surrounding culture, at least in North American affluence, tends to see religious experience itself as one pathway on the quest for self-fulfillment.

When the practices of faith, hope, and compassion are thus regarded, then the whole pattern of religious affections belonging peculiarly to Christianity is radically challenged, not by denial but by affirmation! The idea of acquiring and practicing "holy fear of God" as the beginning of wisdom, however, is surely not immediately self-fulfilling. The popular psychologies of self-actualization leave little room for such reverence or "fear and trembling" before the mystery of God. The human depth of Christ's cry of abandonment on the cross simply cannot be made to fit with my own psychological progress toward wholeness. To live into the pattern of Christian affections runs counter to a view of life which is primarily oriented to "feelings" and behavioral adjustments to the prevailing sentiments of society. What emerges is a very different picture of the human self in relation to community, and finally, a very different notion of human happiness and maturity.

The way of prayer, together and alone, requires a truthfulness in the inmost being which disposes all our social relationships in light of the passion for God: for love of God and neighbor in all things. The affections such as joy, peace, and gladness as experiences in our lives are desirable. There is no sense denying that we do in fact seek these; unless one is consumed by self-hatred or despair, we all seek happiness and emotional well-being.

A life characterized by such affectional dispositions is certainly more desirable than one in which a person is continually jealous, angry, bitter, or self-pitying. Who among us is not drawn to a form of life in which gratitude and compassion are evident? In this sense we may indeed seek happiness and fulfillment through the practice of such affections. Yet the "blessedness" of which Scripture and the great spiritual traditions speak is not simply human self-fulfillment decorated with religious language. With strenuous forms of prayer elicited with the Christian life, happiness and emotional depth are simply not the same as being of a sunny disposition, or of being well-born, well-bred, and in fortunate circumstances.

For such persons, it would seem, human fulfillment is natural and also circumstantial. but the natural gladness of the fortunate having just won the lottery, or having sustained good physical appearance as one ages should not be confused with the joy and gladness of a faithful life over time. Nor should the natural pity for those less fortunate (the "underprivileged," as we say) be confused with compassion learned through pain and suffering and joy in light of what God effects in real life. Within the Christian life, gratitude and gladness and joy are meant to keep company with a sense of incompleteness and brokenness and mortality. The fruits of the Spirit are not simply hopeless ideals we cannot sustain. Rather, they are capacities to live and to sense the world, and to intend and to act in the world born out of mystery and suffering. The Christian life tempers the affections by focusing on the pattern discerned in the humanity of Jesus of Nazareth called the Christ. None of us can jump out of our cultural skins to go back to an easier time (as though we could live a Christian life without engaging our own time and place). So prayer and the religious affections are always culturally embedded and culturally embodied. This also requires respect and receptivity toward differing cultural manifestations of the Christian affections and virtues.

Thus, on the one hand, we must learn from the critics of Christianity - whether theological or social/cultural - to approach the relationship between praying and being with non-presumptive hearts and minds. At the same time, we must never lose sight of the distinctiveness of the affections formed by the stories, ritual practices and most mature examples of liturgical and devotional prayer belonging to the Christian tradition. We are called to seek out a form of life together in which the pattern of distinctively Christian affections is possible. This requires discipline, prayer, common worship, engagement in the world of suffering, ambiguity and mystery. So our gratitude and love, and our cries for mercy and justice co-mingle in a world of terrifying oppression and unbelievable beauty and grace.

The Christian affections are real and authentic only when our lives are grounded in the self-giving of God in the flesh. The natural language of the ˙ heart is something we acquire by living in this world. The language of religious affections requires dwelling with the Word of God in Scripture, prayer, and liturgy. Only open hearts and hands receive the self-giving God whose Word became flesh and whose Spirit animates and sanctifies all things. True prayer sanctifies the sons and daughters of God when it becomes their living idiom. True prayer is also the most primary of theological acts: for it focuses human existence as the ultimate object of all affections.

Notes

Preface

1. Robert C. Roberts, *Spirituality and Human Emotion,* (Grand Rapids: Wm.B. Eerdmanns, 1982), p. 1.
2. Roberta C. Bondi, *To Love As God Loves*, (Philadelphia: Fortress Press, 1987), pp. 107-108.

Chapter 1
Religious Affections Revisited

1. Leo Tolstoy, *A Confession, The Gospel in Brief,* and *What I Believe*, trans. Aylmer Maude (London: Oxford University Press, 1940), p. 5.
2. By Andrew Greeley and William McCready in the *New York Times Magazine*, January 26, 1975.
3. Jacques Ellul, *Prayer and Modern Man,* trans. C. F. Hopkin (New York: Seabury Press, 1973), especially the opening chapter.
4. Jonathan Edwards, *Treatise Concerning Religious Affections*, ed. John E. Smith (New Haven: Yale University Press, 1959), p. 101.
5. *Ibid.*, p. 120.
6. Cf. *The Rule of St. Benedict*, Chapter 20.
7. Edwards, *Treatise Concerning the Religious Affections*, p. 118.
8. *Ibid.*, p. 98.
9. We are not here directly concerned with the question of which emotions must precede or follow another in the actual development of faith. Thus a pattern among the affections, as I will make clear in chapter 4, is not a chronological point but a matter of the order principle in life. The affections hang together in a certain way in Christianity in comparison with others religious traditions. But even within Christian traditions, we can detect differing attempts to ''pattern'' the emotions: e.g. law before Gospel, thus conviction of sin and guilt before joy and thanksgiving.
10. There is a connection between my exploration of the religious affections and issues belonging to the general education of human emotions. This latter topic has surfaced recently in moral philosophy, particularly among those concerned with moral development. We cannot explore in these pages the intersection between moral development and the education of religious affections, but it is important to note a convergence of interest in these two lines of inquiry upon education of the emotions.

   Understanding our inquiry depends in part upon an empathy for questions concerning the human passions, emotions, and feelings in the more general context of moral sensitivity. As John MacMurray observed, ''The education of the emotions . . .consists in the cultivation of a direct sensitiveness to the reality of the world. . . .But in practice sensitiveness hurts. It is not possible to develop the capacity to see beauty without developing also the capacity to see ugliness, for they are the came capacity. The capacity for joy is also the capacity for pain. . . .That is the dilemma in which life has placed us (*Reason and Emotion* [London: Faber and Faber Ltd., 1962], p. 47).

11. Immanuel Kant is perhaps the classic instance in his *Religion Within the Limits of Reason Alone.* The appearance of subjective aims in the moral life leads, for him, to a mixed or inauthentic will.

12. Edwards, *Treatise Concerning the Religious Affections*, p. 98.

13. Richard R. Neibuhr, *Experiential Religion* (New York: Harper & Row, 1972), p. 45. This book is one of the most significant recent attempts to renew and reorient theological thinking to the centrality of the emotions. Neibuhr's concern is much broader and more sensitive to the secular environment or religious faith than my book seeks to be.

14. Paul L. Holmer, "Theology and Emotions," unpublished paper, p. 4.

Chapter 2
PRayeR as the Language of the HeaRt

1. Miguel De Unamuno, *Tragic Sense of Life,* trans. J. E. Crawford Flitch (New York: Dover Publications, 1954), p. 193.

2. In what follows I am particularly indebted to many conversations with Professor Paul Holmer and to his unpublished essay, "The Human Heart: The Logic of a Metaphor."

3. Søren Kierkegaard, *The Concept of Dread*, trans. Walter Lowrie (Princeton, NJ: Princeton University Press, 1946), p. 26.

4. This point could be expanded at great length. My purpose here is to show that, even in a simple case of believing and fearing, what we believe requires that we have certain emotional capacities. That particular emotions and beliefs are reciprocal and may be ingredient in one another is a feature of life which is far more common than we first suppose. My example is based upon a remark of Wittgenstein's: "The belief that fire will burn me is of the same kind of fear that it will burn me." He is focusing upon a kind of certainty shown in both the belief and the emotion. See Ludwig Wittgenstein, *Philosophical Investigations*, trans. G. E. M. Anscombe (Oxford: Basil Blackwell, 1963), ¶ 473, p. 134e.

5. This is the traditional "Collect for Purity," one of Thomas Cranmer's exquisite gifts in translation, retained in the new *Book of Common Prayer* as the opening prayer of the first eucharistic rite. It is widely used in several Christian traditions, most notably by Methodists.

6. Romans 8:19

Chapter Three
Prayer: Shaping and Expressing Emotion

1. Huub Oosterhuis, *Your Word Is Near,* trans. N. D. Smith (Paramus, NJ: Paulist-Newman, 1973).
2. C. S. Lewis, *Surprised by Joy,* (New York: Harvest Books, Harcourt, Brace and World, 1955), p. 61.
3. Martin Luther, *Larger Catechism,* trans. and ed. Robert H. Fischer (Philadelphia: Fortress Press, 1959), III, 26; p. 67.
4. This is discussed in detail in the next chapter in the section, "Gratitude and Giving Thanks."
5. St. Augustine, *Our Lord's Sermon on the Mount,* trans. Francine Cardman in *The Preaching of Augustine,* ed. Jaroslav Pelikan, Preacher's Paperback Library (Philadelphia: Fortress Press, 1973), II, 3:14; pp. 105-106.
6. Cyprian, *De Dominica Oratione,* trans. T. Herbert Bindley, *St. Cyprian on the Lord's Prayer* (London: SPCK, 1914).
7. Origen, *Peri Euches,* chapter xii, *Origen's Treatise on Prayer,* trans. Eric. G. Jay (London: SPCK, 1954), pp. 114-115.
8. Cf. Romans 8:26-27.
9. C. S. Lewis, *Letters to Malcolm: Chiefly on Prayer* (New York: Harvest Books, Harcourt Brace Jovanovich, 1963), p. 82.
10. See my discussion in chapter 2 on the Collect for Purity.
11. *Morning Praise and Evensong* (Notre Dame, IN: Fides, 1973), p.23.
12. This poem is quoted on p. vii.
13. St. Cyprian, *op. cit.*

Chapter Four
The Christian Affections

1. Romano Guardini, *Prayer in Practice,* trans. Prince Leopold of Lowenstein-Wertheim (New York: Pantheon Books, 1957), p. 96.
2. *Ibid.,* p. 98.
3. These examples are from the A. L. Williams translation of the *Berekah Tractate of the Mishnah,* cited in chapter 4 of Louis Bouyer's *Eucharist: Theology and Spirituality of the Eucharistic Prayer,* trans. Charles U. Quinn (Notre Dame:University of Notre Dame Press, 1968).
4. C. S. Lewis, *Reflections on the Psalms* (New York: Harcourt, Brace and World, 1958), p. 94.
5. *Ibid.,* p. 95.
6. Karl Barth, *Church Dogmatics* IV/1, trans. G. W. Bromiley (Edinburgh: T. and T. Clark, 1957), pp. 41-42.
7. *Ibid.,* p. 41-42.
8. Lewis, *Reflections,* p. 96.

9. *Ibid.*

10. Daniel 9:30, Grail translation. Compare its affinities with Psalms such as 118 and 136.

11. Psalm 111:9b-10.

12. Isaiah 6:3, 5.

13. Isaiah 45:15.

14. Hebrews 10:31.

15. St. Bernard of Clairvaux, *Sup. Cant.* 23.14.

16. Hebrews 12:28-29.

17. Max Scheler, "Repentance and Rebirth," *On The Eternal in Man,* trans. Bernard Noble (Hamden, CT: Archon Books, 1971), p. 53.

18. Karl Barth, *Church Dogmatics,* II/1, p. 655.

19. St. Thomas Aquinas, *In Evangelio Joannis.*

20. Edwards, *Treatise Concerning the Religious Affections,* pp. 107-108.

21. C. S. Lewis, *The Weight of Glory and Other Addresses* (New York: Macmillan Publishing Company, 1949), p. 15.

22. Robert Roberts, Kierkegaard on Becoming An 'Individual,' " *Scottish Journal of Theology* 31:147.

Chapter Five
Praying and Thinking: The Work of Theology

1. *The Art of Prayer: An Orthodox Anthology,* trans. E. Kadloubovsky and E. M. Palmer (London: Faber and Faber Ltd., 1951), p. 208.

2. Ignatius of Antioch, *Ad. Magn.*, 8.2.

3. I have in mind Karl Barth and Hans Urs von Balthasar. Of course not every book of theirs is characterized by an equal attentiveness to prayer. Yet their capacity to think in the context of unfolding spiritual insight is unquestionable. This is particularly evident in von Balthasar's book, *Prayer,* trans. A. V. Littledale (New York: Paulist Press, 1967).

4. "The Teaching of the Twelve Apostles," commonly known as The *Didache,* chapter 10; from *Prayers of the Eucharist, Early and Reformed,* trans. R. C. D. Jasper and G. J. Cuming (London: Collins, 1975), p. 15.

5. St. Bernard of Clairvaux, *De consideratione,* 5.30, cited by J. Leclercq, *The Love of Learning and the Desire for God,* trans. C. Misrahi (New York: Fordham University Press, 1961), p.217.

6. Karl Barth, *Evangelical Theology, An Introduction,* trans. Grover Foley (New York: Holt, Rinehart & Winston, 1963), p. 164.

7. Gregory the Great, quoted by an unknown fourteenth-century monk of Farne. Cf. W. A. Pantin, "The Monk-solitary of Farne," *English Historical Review* (1944), cited by Jean Leclercq, *The Love of Learning and the Desire for God.*

8. Louis Bouyer, *Introduction to Spirituality*, trans. Mary P. Ryan (Collegeville, MN: Liturgical Press, 1961), p. 45.

9. Evagrius Ponticus, *The Praktikos: Chapters on Prayer,* 60, trans. with introduction by John Eudes Bamberger (Spencer, MA:Cistercian Publications,1970), p. 65.

Chapter Six
PRaying and Being: Responding in the World

1. Anthony Bloom, *Living Prayer* (Springfield, IL: Templegate Publishers, 1966), p. 128.

2. John Berryman, "Certainly before Lunch," in *Delusions, Etc.* (New York: Farrar, Straus and Giroux, 1972), p. 65.

3. John 17:15. It is fascinating to study the history of interpretation of this text (and the whole of John 17), noting the ever-shifting emphasis in each age to and away from the "this worldly" accent in this prayer.

4. Bloom, *Living Prayer*, p. 62. Bloom uses the term "emotion" here to refer almost exclusively to feelings and to "experienced" passions.

5. Hebrews 11:4.

6. Charles Williams, *Descent of the Dove* (New York: Meridan Books, 1956), p.25.

7. Urban Holmes, "A Taxonomy of Contemporary Spirituality," in *Christians at Prayer,* ed. John Gallen (Notre Dame: University of Notre Dame Press, 1977), pp. 26-45.

8. Bloom, *Living Prayer,* p. 64. Italics and punctuation are his.

9. Most of the early treatises on prayer make this point forcefully. Cyprian, in *De Domenica Oratione,* stresses the communal nature of Christian prayer, even when one prays alone:

    Before all things the Teacher of peace and Master of unity is unwilling for prayer to be made singly and individually, teaching that he who prays is not to pray for himself alone. For we do not say, My Father Who art in heaven, nor Give me this day my daily bread, nor does each one ask that his own debt only be remitted. . . .Prayer with us is public and common: and when we pray, we do not pray for one but for the whole people, because we the people are one. (*St. Cyprian on the Lord's Prayer*, ed. and trans. T. Herbert Bindley [London: SPCK, 1914]. p. 26.)

10. Karl Barth, *Evangelical Theology, An Introduction,* p. 38.

11. *Ibid.*, p. 38.

12. Karl Rahner, *The Church and the Sacraments*, (New York: Herder and Herder, 1963), p.18.

13. Origen's *Treatise on Prayer,* ed. and trans. Eric George (London: SPCK, 1954), p. 115.

14. Two provocative essays on the idea of prayer as a ''not-doing'' or ''useless'' activity are: Nathan Mitchell, ''Useless Prayer'' in *Christians at Prayer*, ed. John Gallen (Notre Dame: Notre Dame University Press, 1977); and David Burrell, ''Prayer as the Language of the Soul,'' in *Soundings* (Winter, 1971), pp. 388-400.

15. Irenaeus, *Contra Haereses*, IV 20:7.

16. Jacques Ellul, *Prayer and Modern Man,* trans. C. Edward Hopkin (New York: Seabury Press, 1973), p. 68.

17. Henri J. M. Nouwen, *Reaching Out: The Three Movements of the Spiritual Life* (Garden City: Doubleday, 1975), p. 97.

18. P. Jecquemont, ''Is Action Prayer?'' in *Concilium*, Vol. 79 (New York: Herder and Herder, 1972), p. 51.

19. von Balthasar, *Prayer*.

20. Gerard Manley Hopkins, ''God's Grandeur,'' in *Poems of Gerard Manley Hopkins,* 3d ed., ed. W. H. Gardner (New York and London: Oxford University Press, 1948), p. 70.

Chapter Seven

Praying with Christ: Signs of Living Prayer

1. I borrow the phrase ''living reminder'' from Henri Nouwen's illuminating book, *The Living Reminder* (New York: Seabury Press, 1977).

2. von Balthasar, *Prayer,* pp. 23-24.

3. Lewis, *Letters to Malcolm*, p. 82.

4. Thomas Merton, *Spiritual Direction and Meditation* (Collegeville: Liturgical Press, 1960), p. 546.

5. *Ibid.*, pp. 57-58.